PRAISE FOR
And Then We Wrote

"ONE AFTER ANOTHER, LIKE STOPPING POINTS ALONG A WINDING MOUNTAIN PATH, the stories and poems in this remarkable collection invite us to pause, breathe, take in new vistas, encounter alternative horizons — to open our eyes and our minds onto unique insights into the complexity of apparently ordinary life. Ranging widely and wonderfully from intimate reminiscences to incisive social commentary to philosophical contemplations and much more, *And Then We Wrote* is a generous anthology of works from writers who share their wisdom with beauty, grace, poignance, and humor."

— *Janise Hurtig*, Community Writing Project and
DePaul University

"THE GRANT STREET WRITERS GENTLY EXPLORE our common humanity through wry humor and great compassion. Meet Crispy and Clean Dean as they attempt to ace a history final. Mourn the loss of Uncle Billy. Explore the landscapes of youth and old age so richly etched in words. Discover how poetry sings through rhyme and form — fixed and free. Go ahead. Pull up a chair or sink back into a pillow with this book. You are now among friends."

— *Jenene Ravesloot*, Author of *Sliders*

"A DELIGHTFUL VIGNETTE OF ALL OUR FAVORITE THINGS we missed during the quarantine: the taste of a tangy margarita in the heat of Mexico, a crowded family visit in a tight Chinatown apartment, a finger licking time spent in Grandma's busy kitchen, a gritty diner and the familiar clang of hurried dishes, an Ethiopian chapel, the bustle of a Mahjong game, and a wave of a magic wand at a granddaughter's birthday."

— *Yvonne Wolf*, Community Producer and
Host of Glenview TV *Off the Shelf*

"THIS COLLECTION IS LIKE A MIXED BOX OF CHOCOLATES, each piece an individual delight. Writing should evoke a kaleidoscope of emotion and what really gets me is authenticity, when you feel the real. I know good writing when I think: I wish I wrote this. When my heart sighs yes, oh no, and please more. That was my reaction.

A yellow highchair, a dresser full of panties, two young boys choking on rollups, a celebration of John Lewis, are just a few images that rocked my world. Do not deny yourself, these sweet pieces can break hearts. Like the queen with her hats, select your delight; you'll be hard-pressed to pick a favorite. Find your 'Comfort Bowl'."

— *Donna Pecore*, Facilitator and
Award-winning Poet and Writer

"*AND THEN WE WROTE* ... AND INDEED THEY DID. The new work by The Grant Street Writers takes each of us by the hand and walks us through family dinners, personal quirks, poetic flights of fancy, special garments, dreams, and compromises. Each author creates a space to explore thoughts, feelings, and resentments; things left undone; accomplishments; resolutions. Whether artistic license or a real look at the individual or relationships steeped in honesty and self-understanding, treat yourself to a truly experiential journey with which to identify, to muse and to glean the meaning of empathy, humor and living life in all its creative fullness."

— *elyse koren-camarra*, Roosevelt University

ALSO BY THE GRANT STREET WRITERS

Wednesdays with Winston

AND THEN WE *wrote*

MORE PROSE AND POETRY

THE GRANT STREET WRITERS

And Then We Wrote: More Prose and Poetry

First Edition

Copyright © 2022 by Grant Street Publishing

Introduction Copyright © 2022 by Ann Fiegen

Front cover photo Copyright © 2022 by Ann Fiegen

Original artwork Copyrighted material by Daniel Cleary, Pages 88, 167, 200; Trudi Goodman, Page 65; Tony Piggott, Page 215; Anne Sylvan, Page 257

Permission for use of original artwork by creator Sandra Belford, Page 4

Photography is the property of respective owners: Marie Davidson, Page 37; Catherine W. Davis, Page 148; Ann Fiegen, Page 113; Fumiko Tokunaga Jensen, Page 118; Judy SooHoo, Pages 242, 278

ISBN: 978-0-9997195-2-7 (print)
ISBN: 978-0-9997195-3-4 (ebook)

Published by The Grant Street Writers

Cover and book design by Phillip Gessert

Printed in the United States of America

To writing groups everywhere, where we go for
support, education and inspiration, and without
whom we would never have found one another

Table of Contents

1   Previously appeared in *Love, Death, and Everything in Between* by the Budlong Woods Writers, 2021

2   Previously appeared in *Tchotchkes* by the Budlong Woods Writers, 2019

Introduction

Wednesdays with Winston was the first publication of The Grant Street Writers. In the years since, there have been many changes. Winston, our furry mascot left in pursuit of The Rainbow Bridge. Our group expanded to include six additional writers, who contribute greatly to diversity in both writing styles and genres as well as gender. On a grander scale, our country was shaken to her core by civil unrest and political divisiveness, and we have all experienced the life-shattering realities of a global pandemic that made fear, sadness and isolation integral components of every day.

We have coped in different ways. Fearing the worst and hoping for the best, we hunkered down in our homes, participated in Zoom meetings instead of social interaction, pursued projects and activities to pass the time and exercise our physical and mental faculties, and struggled with the anonymity imposed by a world of masked faces and social distance.

We have been sustained by a renewed reverence for the simple things. A walk on the beach, observance of the activities of birds, squirrels, chipmunks, the sound of rain on the roof and the smell of the earth after a storm, the glory of a garden in bloom, the magic of an orchestral score, and the magnificence of sunsets all have taken on new meaning.

As writers, we also took pen to paper and wrote of things both relevant and divergent to help us get through it all. We, all of us, took so much for granted, lived our lives without thinking it could ever change, but then it did, and then we wrote, *And Then We Wrote.*

Tim Andersen

Introductory Words

I started writing poetry in first grade and still write poetry 60+ years later. When I think back, I had support every step of the way — from elementary school through high school. I tried out every type of form I came across. When I became comfortable with the rules of the sonnet or the sestina, I looked for ways to break those rules or ignore them altogether. I am also a big fan of humorous verse.

NoDoz & NyQuil

Crispy's real name was Chris. He got his nickname because he consumed copious quantities of weed. Clean Dean got his moniker because he was OCD all the way. Unlike most of the guys on campus, he was the opposite of a college slob. He was so fussy and persnickety that at times he was impossible to deal with. You couldn't touch a cover in his album collection. You couldn't crack the cover of one of his books to look something up. God forbid if you made a condensation ring on his desk with your beer can. Crispy and Clean Dean were the unlikeliest of friends and both excelled on the swim team: Crispy, with his killer crawl, and Clean Dean with his acrobatic dives from the 3-meter board.

They also caroused around town, skipped classes, and didn't do much homework. Then finals rolled around. They decided to pull an all-nighter studying, went to the 24-hour truck stop on the edge of town and bought a box of NoDoz. They looked at the directions, decided they could handle more than the recommended dosage, and each took six. After a while, they didn't feel so hot.

Crispy started complaining that his stash ran out. Even the reliable townie he bought from couldn't get his hands on anything, not even Ditch Weed, a popular strain at the time. The townie told Crispy that it was just one of those periods when supply dries up. Crispy just kept going on and on about how he needed to mellow out from the NoDoz. Clean Dean finally had enough of Crispy's meltdown and started screaming at him to shut the hell up. The textbooks on their respective desks lay unopened.

They went back to the truck stop to buy NyQuil to help them unwire. They finally crashed as the sun was coming up and missed their history final. They asked Mr. Clarkson, their history professor, if they could make up the test. He said No, that missing a final without some sort of prior communication was an automatic 'F'.

Clean Dean came up with a plan. They would appeal to Mr. Case, their swim team coach. Everyone knew that Mr. Clarkson and Mr. Case were best buds. Mr. Case called Crispy and Clean Dean lots of unflattering names, then told them he would speak to Mr. Clarkson. Mr. Case was able to get the test rescheduled on condition of total secrecy.

Crispy and Clean Dean both got a 'D' on the test but were able to stay on the swim team. They spilled the beans at a party, which led to an investigation of a cheating scandal in the athletic department, which got Mr. Clarkson and Mr. Case fired.

Clean Dean continued cleaning his room. Crispy finally scored some weed.

Tim Andersen

Seining For Minnows in Iowa

Why buy minnows when you can seine?
Seining worked best when it was rainy

We dragged our nets across the bottom of a creek
If we got shut out, my dad had a fit of pique

If we got a lot of minnows, we went fishing
We fished for bullhead. They looked like mini catfish.

We curled our hooks through each minnow's spine
1 day we caught 4 dozen bullhead. Man did we dine!

We also caught bluegill, crappie, bass and perch
My dad told our dinner guests about the black birch

grove on Spirit Lake. He said There's a lawn
right on the water. Cast out at dawn,

which was a fib. We fished off a dock at dusk.
They left. He said I ain't telling everyone my stuff.

And you shouldn't either.
Take a breather.

And Then We Wrote

My dad was a career field superintendent
He came from nothing and transcended

and became that guy with a Mexican crew
who built churches and schools

in Houston. The field super is so vital
that he or she should be entitled

to recognition of fixing then executing
faulty plans from the architect that require resolution.

But enough about seining.
I'm not complaining. I'm just explaining.

The Buckinghams

I was 10 or maybe 12
but I had to shelve

my desire to see The Buckinghams
at the Roof Garden in Arnolds Park because

I was too young. Damn it!
Then I heard chitchat about

how The Buckinghams were arrested for possession
of marijuana during a jam session

right there at the Roof Garden in Arnolds Park!
That was the first time I heard that word and it sparked

my interest. There were no repercussions
for The Buckinghams because Northwest Iowa was

predominantly Scandinavian and looked at pot
the same way they looked at aquavit:

They're a lenient bunch. Here's a warning
Sleep it off until morning.

And Then We Wrote

I saw The Buckinghams 40 years later as the headliner
for a summer event in Jefferson Park.

A group of women knew the words to every song
and waved their fan club banner all day long.

Between the joints selling food
and the joints being lit,

The Buckinghams never sounded better
and Jefferson Park never smelled better.

Facebook

My mom is in her
80s I am in my
60s and combined

we bore everyone
on Facebook
Mom posts pictures of cats

I post pictures of food
This is Kat playing writes mom
This is a pork chop I write

but what I didn't write is that I marinated that pork chop in
soy sauce, lime juice, garlic and brown sugar overnight then
cooked that pork chop in a pan in New Orleans in a shabby
house on Chartres Street where the neighborhood is noisy
and there's a factory across the street that starts up at 5 am
and there are trains that go by at all hours of the day and
night but I like it because I've got the travel bug. I spent a
month in Montana, two months in Texas, three months in
Italy, four months in New Orleans. In the future I want to
drink sake in Tokyo, soju in Seoul, beer with the blokes in
Melbourne. Life used to be a jet plane getting from Point A
to Point B as fast as possible but now it's a tramp steamer
pulling into ports of call after spending days adrift.

This is Kat drawing
a bath writes mom
This is a unicorn cutlet

I write Mom's grandkids
hit the Like button at the
fantastical and magical

efforts of their grandma
and her son's
old people antics

Kat sets the table
I make eggs and toast
Mom takes a picture
then hits Post

Charm School

I was the only guy. I got hired as a snobby sentry
but had to learn about entry

into society. Deportment?
I thought I was getting deported

to where
I had no idea but figured I was going there

but no. It had to do with etiquette
and how to make an omelet.

I signed up because I thought it was going to be a salon
filled with bons vivants.

I didn't exactly flunk.
The school just went defunct.

I transferred to BrilliantOut
where I was the idiot savant

of polite society. I studied at Beaux Chadre.
I studied at Vieux de Chalet.

And Then We Wrote

Then I got hired by the mob.
How did I get that job?

I could type thousands of words
a day for that nasty turd

who hired me to transcribe
his scribbles describing his bribing

of officials
and though tempted to blow the whistle,

I didn't. Which witch or warlock amidst and amongst us
authorized those ridiculous Rules of Etiquette
    in the first place

and why am I sad that said rules no longer exist?
Charm school closed around the same time

that politeness was poisoned and dumped in a ditch.
In the battle between the light and bright forces of good

against the dark forces of evil, evil is winning
and I thought Alrighty then.

Dreamy

A dream during showers
brought enthusiasm at its recall.
Crucial edges of twilight
hampered conscientiousness and vexed

a deal describing the dream's meaning.
Anyhow, slumber turned into a crater
filling with reduplicated scenes
of slight deviations like a freighter

going from place to place then back again,
repetitive yet different every time.
Draw a blank when you wake. There were
imaginary commitments made by two-bit, dime

store, kid-game playing stupid shits,
stoned and drunk, but tons of fun to be around,
kind of dreamy and married to the concept
that nothing they think or do has consequences.

A deserted strip mall sat in front of them.
There was no legal means for getting in.
On the other hand, it wasn't guarded.
Drab-ash dawn was streaming into

souls, leaving a smudge. In the 3rd
decade of the 21st century, evidence of fun
exists although scarce. Nobody can stop their
gliding into this inelegant, decaying shell

of emptiness on this gray fall day.
Their movement scars the gray flat layers
of primordial dust. The badass vests
bearing snakes and skulls do not awaken

the dream that is going wrong.
Thankfully, the alarm interrupts the dream
that was starting to last too long.

I Hated Malaga

I went there to forget
but I ended up remembering
what I didn't want to remember.

This dream came back to me.
An owl had its talons around my wrist.
I punched it in the face

and knocked over
a big green plastic glass of water
sitting on the dresser by the side of the bed.

The next night an owl
had me around the forearm.
I grabbed its neck

and shoved his face in the sand
until I let go and woke up
with a fistful of pillow

and fell back to sleep an hour later.
Mostly my dreams involve someone
or something chasing me.

Like dogs or mutants.
Sometimes I'm running down a fire escape.
I told a woman in Malaga named Rosie

about my dreams. She asked me questions
about my life. No one had ever asked me
about my life. No one before her ever gave a shit.

I told my drug dealer
about bowling a 700 series.
His response was that he just wowed the crowd

playing guitar at an open mike.
"You shoulda seen me," he said. "I killed it!"
He doesn't give a shit about anything except himself.

He threw a party. I was invited so I went.
I overheard a conversation.
It turned out that the people he invited

didn't give a shit about him.
They only showed up because they were invited.
I found out later that not giving a shit

is a medical condition. It's actually a boil.
Not on the outside like eczema
but on the inside where there is no cure.

I went into a Catholic Church in Malaga and said "God
Is there no psalm that can reach
your radiant draconian high-rise of incommunicadoness?"

The luminosity of intrepid congregations
standing sitting kneeling standing sitting kneeling
like performance artists in a museum

is fading away while illicit hot sex
in the hellfire of an afternoon
is blossoming

which reminded me of my big-titted ex-girlfriend
who I never think of
but one day I heard her name on TV.

It was a transmission that bled into my ears
and through the walls of my thick skull.
A newscaster was criticizing her answer to a question.

"I remember her," I thought.
Once upon a time she slapped me
when her roommate sat on my lap at a party.

Her roommate's cashmered arm
enveloped my neck and ran up and down my back.
The naked bulb in the streetlight outside the ex-girlfriend's

picture window made a halo around her pissed off self.
It was a night at a party long forgotten
and now an unwanted memory that I voided and vacated

years and years ago, a memory that I wanted
to please stay away, so except for the friendly people,
the perfect weather, the picture postcard fantastical scenery,

the food, especially the Jamón Ibérico and the Manchego,
and the wine, especially the local rioja,
I hated Malaga.

Hamlet's Soliloquy > an Andersenella

I saw my dead father upon the parapet and thought
I'm dreaming. It's but a dreaming bother. Why fret? And yet
he was killed by my uncle who was banging mother though
he was like a brother to me. To act or not to act.
That really is the question. So I consulted with my staff
and affirmed more questions. Is it better to let things go?
This is gritty business. Or should I put up a fight or
barge in on him at his place of business to frighten him,
yell at him and let him know the current state of affairs
is not right? I could just kill him but myself would suffer.
The DA would say, "Yourself killed Uncle." And I would say
"Yeah, I snuffed him out" then would weep in a cell in
    hell for
what I'd done, trying to forget the threat of what's ahead.

We are either

going to heaven or
going to hell or
going to purgatory or
going to lie in the earth or
going to have our ashes scattered or
going to a funeral pyre

The outcome is hopeless despite the dressings, the blessings,
e.t.c. When I was on death row, the family could
only come to visit according to rules made by old
white fools who don't have a clue that family still matters.
Those in charge of visitation are doing as little
as possible as befits their station because they've seen
it all before so when you show up because you have a
loved one in a cell and you're stressed out, they point
    to a door
and seem extraordinarily disrespectful. Our
lack of knowledge of death — a loss of breath then
    a black hole —
makes us stupider than Cupid who slings divorce darts at
our hearts. Is sturdy work as a clerk better or worse than
thoughtful art? No answer there but it is the start
    of thoughts.

Tides turn. A call will come where views unfold.

About the Author

Tim Andersen has published poems in many poetry magazines over the last 45 years. He has published two books: *Jet Plane* and *Nine*. Besides reading and writing, he likes to travel, cook, play bridge and bowl.

Marie Davidson

Introductory Words

While I have always wanted to be a writer, for many years my personal writing was mainly confined to journals. Some years ago, after I ripped out a small stack of pages to save, I shredded all of them. I did not want my repetitive complaining to be my writing legacy. I labored under the mistaken idea that "real" writers write fiction. Fiction, however, did not come easily to me. After taking a class in personal essay writing, I had an epiphany — my own life was a lot more interesting than anything I could make up! I discovered my natural resource, the narrative memory of a storyteller. Just about anything can make a good story and, if there is a humorous angle, so much the better. The Grant Street Writers have inspired me to try writing poetry, a wonderfully condensed way to express what is personal and true.

Life Lessons at the Randolph

In the spring of 1977, I moved to Chicago to be with my then-boyfriend. I had five months to fill in before I started a Ph.D. program in psychology at the University of Illinois. I needed a job and I was not picky. Thanks to Mrs. Domowski at the Illinois Department of Employment, I was sent to the Randolph Inn for an interview for a waitressing job. The Randolph was a busy restaurant in Chicago's Loop, serving breakfast and lunch customers and a smaller dinner crowd.

George, one of the Greek owners, sat me down in a booth, looked at me sternly, and said, "You have experience?" I had decided that my experience serving food once a week at the family-style dinners in my dorm during freshman year should count. I said, "Yes." And that was it. George beckoned to another waitress. "Harriet, come here and tell her where to buy a uniform." Stunned by this rapid hiring process, I asked, "When do you want me to start?" George looked at me with suspicion. "Tomorrow."

And so began my first and last career experience as a waitress. The high of the job was realizing, after a time, that I could live anywhere and make a very modest living as long as my feet held up. The low of the job was realizing that I was not very good at it. The only other job I'd had that was as physically demanding was the summer I worked as a nurse's aide at Boston Children's Hospital. But then I was taking care of sick kids and, to some extent, their worried parents.

31

There was honor in that work, however menial. The work of a waitress does not come automatically with honor or glory. It comes with abuse from bosses and cooks; being hit on by jerks who see a waitress as prey for lustful advances; and at the end of the day, splitting your tips with the busboys who made your job manageable. It was then you would recall with some bitterness the tightwads who left lousy tips, or worse, stiffed you.

My fancy Ivy League education had not prepared me for this experience. And yet, it was probably the perfect experience for someone who was soon to begin the study of clinical and social psychology. Up to then, my jobs had all been in libraries, museums, or in some kind of childcare. Now I was thrown into the wild social microcosm of a restaurant run by Greeks, a staple in Chicago, where it basically came down to kill or be killed. Do I exaggerate? Of course I do, but not by much. Before the Randolph Inn, I'd had a lovely fantasy of one day running a serene bed and breakfast in a small New England town by a lake, where my guests would be fascinating individuals who would adore my delicious and creative food. Two weeks into the job at the Randolph, I knew I would never go anywhere near the food industry for the rest of my life.

I bought a waitress uniform at Wieboldt's, the department store a hostile Harriet had sent me to. She also advised buying good waitress shoes. I got the uniform, a polyester dress that zipped up the front. It was an unattractive mustard yellow. I skipped the shoes, thinking it would be a waste for a five months' job. Wrong! After day one on the job, I limped back to Wieboldt's and bought the white tie-up grandma shoes and I had to admit, damn it, Harriet was right. The only good thing about the uniform was that I could wash it out each night, to get out the smells of cigarettes and fried food that clung to me and my clothes after a day at the Randolph. The dress would almost drip-dry by the next day.

Learning the ropes was a crash course, because once the

customers came flooding in, the show was on and there were hours before any break. I was terrified. What the hell had I done? I was good at greeting people and smiling and being nice, but that is not what they came for. They came to get food and to get it in a very timely way. As the newbie, I got some slack, and a couple of the other waitresses were kind, except Harriet, she was having schadenfreude all over the place, watching me fail. Diane and especially Pat tried to help. "Can I get some pops for your 4-top? Let me show you how to hide some steak knives. George and Andy (the co-owner) are too cheap to have enough." Their kindness kept me going. There had to be honor in this job, goddammit, even if it was my own pride that was in the balance. Maybe something like this had sustained my male friends who went into the Marine Corps through basic training at Parris Island. Was there a waitress battle cry like "Oorah!"? I thought it could be, "Oh feet!"

I survived the first week. George made a point of ostentatiously checking my arithmetic on my first few orders. That part I had down. I figured out the battle plan of the day. Where are my tables? Who is my busboy? What are the specials? How to put in an order, now that was a fracas, on a daily basis. It was all verbal, like being in the pit of the Board of Trade when all the buying and selling was done by yelling. If I had an order for two people it had to be conveyed, clearly in one piece, as "Cheeseburger special medium, up with a Denver with rye toast." Conveyed when there was a break in the cacophony of the other waitresses shouting in their orders, and I often missed the rhythm. That really pissed off Harriet.

For the most part, I was on the lunch and dinner shift. It made it a late night for me to get home but when I was on breakfast and lunch for a few weeks I really hated it. The breakfast customers were in a big rush to get to work, plus they were very fussy. People get wedded to their eggs being cooked just so and the Randolph Inn cooks didn't give a crap about the finer points of eggs. Abuse for me, lousy tip, and not my fault. Lunch time was a total zoo. Dinner was very slow, with only a few diners and a bunch of regulars in the bar.

When I think back on my experience as a pretty lousy waitress at the Randolph Inn, the most vivid memories are of the characters who defined the place for me. And the way it was organized. Owners, cooks, and bartenders, all Greek immigrants, who all seemed to be named George, Andy, Pete, or Nick. Except for Spiros, the poor bastard who had to get up in the middle of the night to buy food at the early morning market. The waitresses were all female and white, except for Louise, a light-skinned African American from Louisville. Louise and I shared the dinner shift, when she gave me wise advice. "Girl, you have to think ahead. I used to be cute and popular like you, and now I need to think of the future, so I have *in*-surance, and I pay that premium every month." Louise also told me I had to root for the "Cubbies" and where to get the best deals in winter coats — the January sales at Montgomery Ward.

The busboys and dishwashers were either Black or Hispanic, seriously underpaid (weren't we all?) and yet they were the fragile underpinning of the whole operation. The basic rule at the Randolph Inn was show up and work hard. This is what makes the world go around, whether you are a rich venture capitalist or a lowly food server.

My favorite customer was Sheldon, the fifty-something, sad sack fellow who came in every morning at 10:45 on a break from his office job at the State of Illinois Building. He was Jewish, garrulous, bigoted, and always pissed off. About everything. I'd pour him a coffee refill and just listen. "They always want more. You give them this (he motions cutting off his hand); then they want this" (he motions cutting off his forearm) — his comment on African Americans. Sheldon's opinion of the Illinois governors he'd served under over the years was, "However you slice it, they are all a bunch of bums on the take." All these years later, who could argue with that observation? Sheldon didn't even like his own background very much. "What is Yiddish? It's not a language, it's a mongrel mishmosh of this and that." I asked him once what made him smile and he said, "You, pouring me coffee."

There was Harriet, the career waitress who just didn't like me. Maybe she sniffed me out right away as a fraud—a college girl posing as a waitress. She really cleaned my clock one morning when she criticized my sloppy preparation of a half grapefruit. She proceeded to show me how to do it correctly, then held it up and said, "See? Pretty as a picture." What could I say but, "You're right, Harriet. Thank you." College girl eats a helping of humble pie.

And Pete, one of the Greek cooks. He was 20 years older than me, a balding married man supporting a family. Every day just before the lunch crowd streamed in, he'd leer at me from his spot at the grill and say. "So, what you say, honey, you and me we go out to Sweetwater tonight (a bar on Rush Street) and have a good time, hey?" click-clicking suggestively with his tongue. About one and a half hours later, at the height of the lunch pandemonium and after a few of my botched orders, Pete's tune changed to, "You stupid bitch! You mess everything up!" (Harriet smiled at this point.) This really did happen, every day. No one thought much of it, including me. But that was then, 40 years ago.

And then there was Pat, the kindest and nicest person in the place and I think of her still as a beacon of warm calm, a bodhisattva of food service. In the post lunch lull, when the servers and helpers could relax and eat a free meal ("No steak! Are you crazy?"— that was Andy the co-owner, after I innocently ordered one my first day on the job), Pat and I would hang out and talk about our lives. It was the superficial yet intimate things female co-workers talk about. One afternoon in August, I saw Pat sitting in a booth, sobbing quietly, shoulders heaving. I sat down next to her. "What's wrong, Pat?" Between gulping sobs, she said, "Elvis is dead. I just found out." I never found out exactly what Elvis had meant to her, but I did my best then to comfort her. The King was dead.

I got to know Gloria and Margaret, two older ladies who

came to the Randolph almost every night for dinner and cocktails, and to wait for the traffic to die down on the Edens Expressway, but it was really to meet and have several cocktails. I waited on them a lot. When I was close to going back to school, I told some of my regulars that I would be leaving. When I told Gloria and Margaret, they asked why, and I said I was going to graduate school. Gloria was very surprised that her waitress was off to graduate school and said, "Well then, you must have gone to college." I said I had, and she tried to guess which college. "Mundelein, right?" naming a local Catholic women's college. I said no, not there, and she asked, "Well. Where then?" I said, reluctantly, "Harvard." After a long pause, and a double take, she said, "THE Harvard?" I gave her a big smile and said, "Is there another one?" One of the few times I have ever admitted to being a Harvard graduate, but Gloria provoked me.

After forty years, The Randolph Inn is no longer there. There is a Randolph Tavern, which seems to be in the same street space and which is definitely an upscale restaurant. It offers small plates that favor "Mediterranean" dishes, but not Greek — there is no moussaka, pastitsio, or gyros on the menu. I wish I knew what happened to the people I spent almost half a year with and where I learned so much about how to live, make a living, and how to listen. When I visited Graceland in 2011, I did a special meditation at Elvis's grave and offered it in honor of Pat, my patron saint of waitressing and teacher in how to be a mensch, as Sheldon might have put it.

Dear Uncle Billy

December, 2019

Dear Uncle Billy,

I have your picture on my desk. It's the same photo that was always on display in the living room of my childhood home. I knew you were special.

On the stairway to my grandmother's second-floor flat, one of those mass-produced paintings hung by the stained-glass window at the bend of the stairs. It was an image of a young sailor with strawberry blond hair. A youthful Jesus with sad eyes had his hand on the sailor's shoulder. I was sure the sailor was you, Uncle Billy. I spent long moments at that bend in the stairway gazing at you and Jesus.

In the photo on my desk, taken just after you enlisted, you are young and handsome, wearing your Navy uniform and a shy smile. Your blue eyes look right at me. That smile reveals a dimple on your right cheek. Your strawberry blond hair is a compact mass of tight curls, your sailor cap just barely visible. You were 20 years old when you joined the Navy. A war was on.

I can't explain why I, the niece you never met, has spent more than 60 years thinking about you and missing you. Growing up, I went to Mass every Sunday with my family at

Saint John Chrysostom Church in Boston. During the prayer for the dead, I remembered you. I spoke your name.

On Memorial Day, I went with your brothers, my father and three uncles, to tend to the family graves. Your remains were not there, although your name was on the headstone. Your remains were deep in the ocean, off the coast of Okinawa. Your ship, the USS *Luce*, sank on May 4, 1945. You were a petty officer, watertender third class. You were below deck when the Japanese planes hit, and you were struck in the head by an air compressor. It was a fatal blow, the family was told. Your shipmates could not even try to save you. They scrambled up the ladder to escape an engine room that was filling with water. You were among the nineteen sailors on the *Luce* killed in action.

My grandmother, your mother, spent many hours on the sofa in her living room, dressed in her drab housecoat, saying the rosary, with beads in one hand and a Salem in the other. I asked her, "Why are you sad, Nana?" Taking a puff of her cigarette, she answered, "I am praying for my dead boy."

I can tell you this, Uncle Billy. You were very loved. I was told that you were the sunshine guy. Always finding a way to be helpful. Aunt Jean, your sister-in-law, said "Billy always had a smile." My mother, who was no fan of her in-laws, told me you were her favorite. One of the tunes she sang as she rolled out pie dough in our downstairs kitchen was the one with the lyrics, "Bell bottom trousers, coat of navy blue, she loves her sailor and he loves her too." I don't know if you even had a sweetheart who grieved for you, Uncle Billy.

You were the uncle who did not come back. Five brothers in the Navy. Four came home, but not you. For me, you will always be twenty-one. I imagine that the two Japanese Kamikaze pilots who hit the USS *Luce* were also very young, and that they were serving their country. They never came back, either, and their bones lie near yours in the East China Sea.
With love,
Marie

Anarchy, My Beloved

"How do you feel about your son being arrested and called an anarchist?"

That was the message a reporter for the *Miami Herald* left on our phone. My husband picked up the message and called me. I was on my way to volunteer at the local high school in an arts fair. I turned around and went home, where we searched the internet for information.

Our 19-year-old son, Ben, had told us he'd be in Miami demonstrating against the 2003 Free Trade Act of the Americas. Thirty-four countries were meeting that November to discuss the treaty, which many social activists believed would only hurt the little guy and benefit big corporations. It was perfectly possible that Ben did see himself as an anarchist, he'd done a lot of reading about it in high school, from Emma Goldman to Noam Chomsky. We found Ben in a photo on the *Miami Herald* website, sitting on the ground with a group of young men, all in handcuffs.

So began the latest chapter in our son's reign of terror — the terror being what he evoked in his parents. After living vicariously through a year of Ben hopping trains coast to coast, his arrest in New York City for panhandling with a night spent in the "Tombs," and his bout of malaria in Mexico, we had developed some coping mechanisms. My husband Irv, Ben's stepdad, went superrational and dove into research. I had embraced Buddhism. Mindful breathing was my go-to practice. "Breathing in, I hold Ben in my heart; breathing out, I send him love and good will." Karma can be a bitch, and I was embracing it.

We were able to find out Ben had been sent to the Dade County Jail and charged with "burglary of an unoccupied structure." Next, we called everyone we could think of for advice. Did he need a defense attorney? Should we find a bondsman to post bail? A friend had a criminal defense attorney acquaintance, Kent. Kent told us that Ben was the wild card in this situation. What did Ben want? If we hired an attorney it would have to be someone in Florida. Kent knew people down there and they were very expensive.

"Don't hire your own attorney. He'll get a public defender. And don't post bail, at least not yet. If the case becomes federal it'll be more serious and we can talk again."

I had a new understanding of the saying, "Why are you making a federal case out of this?" We decided the best course of action was to wait and see. We had not talked to our son yet, and there really wasn't any way to initiate it.

A call came in two days later from a Mr. Pablo Miranda, the assistant public defender assigned to Ben's case. I was touched by his kindness in reaching out to us. Pablo managed to be both reassuring and alarming.

"I saw your son. Ben is fine. He could get up to five years for the charge of felony burglary, but what they actually did was not that serious. Ben was found sleeping in an empty house that was probably abandoned, along with three other guys. They had chains and rubber tubes in the house and the police said they were weapons, but they were supplies for their bicycles. I want to plead this down to a trespassing misdemeanor. Ben could get sixty days or get out with time served."

Pablo said it usually took twenty-one days to get the plea to court and he'd try to move it along faster. He knew the state's attorney on the case and he suggested we call him and say we were hoping Ben would be home for Thanksgiving.

When he gave us the state's attorney's number, he told us not to say where we got it.

We asked about posting bail. Pablo agreed with Kent that might not be a best idea at this point. It was $5000, so he could get out with $500. Pablo thought local bondsmen would be reluctant to do it because Josh was from out of state.

It was actually a good thing, Pablo said, that Ben and his friends were arrested before the demonstration in Miami.

"The police tased demonstrators and when they were convulsing on the ground, the cops took them in for "resisting arrest."

Ben got in touch. He could only call collect and the rate per minute was ridiculous. When I answered the phone, I heard a recorded voice asking, "Will you accept a collect call from Dade County Jail from?" Then a pause, followed by Ben saying, "your favorite son in prison." I wouldn't say he exactly treated jail time like a lark, but clearly, he was fine. His only complaint was that he and his friends were sick of PB&J sandwiches. They had insisted on vegan food and the jail was not a restaurant. He also told us absolutely *not* to post bail. It was a solidarity issue and he didn't want to abandon the three others incarcerated with him.

Of course, I felt a lot better just hearing Ben's voice. Irv resumed research on activist groups. He found the Legal Hotline for FTAA Protestors, and various volunteer legal groups. I tried calling the state's attorney as Pablo had suggested, and received a very chilly response from his assistant, who told me if I wasn't the one pressing charges, it wasn't up to me to decide when my son would get out.

Over the next few weeks there were many calls back and forth with Ben, Pablo, and various legal aid groups. I was on a first name basis with several secretaries. Typical of how the legal system works in Florida, and probably everywhere, the case was continued, no charges were filed for weeks, and clear communications were rare.

Ben got bailed out by a social justice group and went to

stay in Asheville, North Carolina. Pablo said this was not great, because after bail is posted you can't leave the state. Pablo was sure Ben would have to appear in court. I engaged in nail-biting, handwringing, and more Buddhist mindful breathing. In the end, Ben was not required to appear at court in person. All charges were dropped, six and a half weeks after his arrest. Pablo called to give me the good news.

"Yeah, I think the authorities were getting a lot of heat in the press for the way the police beat up people at the protest and decided pursuing charges was not going to be a winner."

I loved Pablo, the public defender who went above and beyond to keep an anxious parent informed.

Before his arrest in the abandoned house, Ben had spent a night in the backyard of a home in Miami. A sympathetic activist couple allowed demonstrators to store their stuff and spend the night. Ben's backpack with his ATM card and passport were stolen. This would soon lead to a lot of red tape, gross bank incompetence, and a very long wait for a new passport. These would be my tasks, as Ben was now on his way to Philadelphia and new activist projects, so not in a position to handle personal business.

I called the phone number of the sympathetic couple — the phone number was another gift from Pablo — to check on the lost backpack. I talked to Marge, an older woman who told me that she and her husband had given up marching in the streets, but still tried to help young people who were fighting for a more just society. Marge said Ben's backpack had not shown up, but she offered me these words from the poet Kahlil Gibran's "On Children" —

Your children are not your children.
They are the sons and daughters of Life's longing for itself.
They come through you but not from you,
And though they are with you, yet they do not belong to you.

I sent Marge a thank you note. I also sent one to Pablo, with a very nice Christmas card.

Security Breach

After 9/11, new rules sprang up around air travel to beef up security, thereby making flying about as much fun as a day traveling on a cramped, bumpy stagecoach. One pleasant custom from the past was eliminated — you could no longer accompany someone to their gate or meet someone at their gate, without getting a special pass. Most airlines allowed for this in the case of minor children, the elderly, or active military.

Three years later, in 2004, I still had not fully adjusted to the new rules. I knew about the rule to not meet people at the gate without special permission and I certainly knew about the long security lines. But when I arrived at American Airlines at O'Hare International Airport to meet my ninety-year-old father's plane coming in from Boston and saw the giant crowds I knew I was in deep trouble. My mistake was to have not left home much earlier. I really had to be at his gate when my father walked off the plane to help him. He was still doing pretty well at age ninety, but he could get disoriented. He had managed to lose his passport on his flight to Dublin two years earlier, and that meant an emergency trip to the American Consulate and a whole lot of stress. Later on, he shook the first passport out of his pants. "Of course, I looked there. It wasn't there then." You can see why I was concerned.

I had two big hurdles before I could get to the airport concourse. The first was getting a security pass. The second was to go through security. It did not help that the damn plane was going to be early. I figured I had about twenty-five minutes tops, to get to the gate. How could I do that with mobs of people ahead of me. There had to be a way.

In the area for obtaining a security pass, the sign read, "Military personnel and their families may go to the head of the line." I casually strolled along the outside of the roped-in line of people waiting and casually attached myself to a military family near the front. I told myself to smile, and to look like you are the loving aunt of this brave young man going to serve in the Air Force. No one said a thing. I dawdled far enough away from the family of the young man so they wouldn't necessarily see me as part of them, but other observers would. Almost to the front of the line, I saw there were three agents issuing special passes. Now it was "our" turn. The family walked up to the open agent, but they had finally noticed me, and gave me a hard look that said, "And who the hell are you, lady?" There was a very awkward space of about a minute when I was just up there at the front of the line alone, but no one challenged me, and I stepped very quickly to the next agent who was open. I explained my request, gave the agent my dad's flight information and my ID and got my pass.

I then skedaddled to the regular security line. Way too long. I switched over to the VIP line, which was moving along smartly. The security agent did not bat an eye when I showed him my ID and my pass. Since I was now a VIP, I did not have to remove my shoes. Wonderful. I got through in minutes, no pat down and no X ray. I checked my watch. Then I checked the flight board. Oh God, dad's plane was at the gate! And it was gate H-18, about as far away as you could be from the main concourse. I put everything my fifty-seven-year-old body had into a manic sprint down the concourse, dodging dozens of chubby Midwesterners moving like snails pulling their carry-ons behind them.

I arrived at H-18 at the precise moment that dear dad was exiting the walkway into the arrival lounge. I waved at him, trying to get my huffing and puffing under control. We hugged. My father said, "You know, the plane was 15 minutes early. I wasn't sure you'd be here." Smiling, I said, "Dad, wild horses couldn't keep me from meeting you at your gate."

The Power of Two

When the union of two souls begins to fray,
With humor and good will in short supply,
No superhero comes to save the day,
And yet there is no thought to say goodbye.

The devil's in the details, that is true,
The single checkbook caused much needless pain.
She estimates; he to the penny hews,
Let's each have one! We then have much to gain.

The doubling up expanded to the tea
kettles, so he got his, she bought her own.
He boiled his water very carefully,
Her kettle sang before the moon was down.

The final step was separate sleeping lairs.
Division was the savior of the pair.

Marie Davidson

In Memoriam: RBG

Jews say the Holy One holds back the best
Until the sunset signals a new year.
Her book is sealed, and now she is at rest.
Those she inspired are filled with dread and fear.

The Ship of State lies rotting in the swamp
Of the Potomac, where the light is out.
A rough beast holds the cards, an angry lump,
The nation stumbles on, led by a lout.

Fires rage, wild tempests batter at our shores,
The Tiny Virus takes a wicked toll.
Each step of daily life feels like a war,
November, we will battle for our souls.

She said, Dissent, and never cease the fight.
We pray with all our strength that she was right.

About the Author

Marie Davidson is a retired librarian and psychologist, which reflects her love of the written word and her wonder at what makes people tick. As a preteen growing up in Boston, she founded The Junior Writers of America. This was a bust, but she never lost her love of writing. She is fascinated by the workings of memory. These words of the writer Louise Penny resonate: "Our lives are shaped by our perceptions, not just by memories, but by how we remember things."

Trudi Goodman

Introductory Words

I have always been interested in true stories. "Life is stranger than fiction." "Stick to the facts." And so on.

Laughing is probably my favorite activity next to dancing, and so my desire to make others laugh is a big part of my life's ambitions. If I have achieved that, I consider it a success story.

Size Chubette

When I was a little girl taking dancing lessons, my mother was always worried about the effect my few pounds over-weight would have on this activity. After my lessons, she would suggest I sit down to recover because according to her, I was *overheating.*

"You might have to quit lessons because you are OVER-HEATING, and this could cause you to catch a cold."

I was considered a fat child. Yes fat, fatty, and fatso were adjectives I got used to hearing. Crying about it was not an option, because crying in my home was not allowed. "There's no crying over spilled milk." Mom's words. "I mean it! No crying in this house."

I had no idea how to get rid of my overweight problem. I also had no idea what dieting meant or cutting down on cal-ories, or "what's a calorie?" By the time I was in high school, five-foot-two me weighed 165 lbs, and I wore a size 17 dress. Nowhere near resembling an American beauty. It seemed like this was the goal set up by the powers-at-large in Hollywood. Whether five foot one or five foot nine, the dress size recom-mended by the movie industry for all girls was size seven, and this should be a loosely fitting garment. Growing up with Lana Turner, Hedy Lamarr, Veronica Lake, just to name some of the Silver Screen beauties, was not beneficial to any young girl weighing more than 110 pounds. And in the forties and fifties, you were only accepted if you were a raven-haired beauty or a blond bombshell. Dishwater blond was a dirty look. The extremes of trying to be somewhat acceptable to be a valued part of the female population was doubly hard on the girls who lacked luster.

My mother, who was desperate to have a pretty child, a svelte girl, decided to take me to her doctor for advice. It was a policy in those days to not coddle the patients. "I'll tell it like it is," said the good doctor. "You are for sure overweight, and an embarrassment to your mother. Shame on you."

It's hard to believe than anyone who signed up to preserve life could have been so uncaring, but he was. And so he sent me home, tossing out some words of wisdom.

"Just stop eating so much."

Given no diet advice or even the knowledge of such a thing, I started to invent possibilities to get the ball rolling. How I ever got this idea is still a mystery to me. I think it might have been an explanation provided on the packaging of a garment called the Playtex 18 Hour Girdle. It advertised a special benefit. The girdle was guaranteed to cause weight loss in the wearer.

I decided to buy the Playtex Girdle. It was made of rubber, a Pepto Bismol-colored rubber with air holes punched throughout. The idea was to wear the girdle as much as possible and to take long walks wearing it, the hotter the day the better. This exercise would create a very sweaty body, and the fat would roll off. For about a month I went along with the game plan.

I walked miles and miles through the city leaving drops of my DNA everywhere until one day welts appeared on my stomach. The sight was so hideous I feared for my life. Besides being fat, I was also a hypochondriac, and when the red blotches showed up, I decided I was risking my life by wearing the girdle. Besides that, I hadn't lost even one pound. And so, I dispensed with the Playtex and moved on to a very popular idea at the time, the egg and grapefruit diet.

This fifties' creation was designed to help burn fat, and

suddenly I was introduced to what dieting was all about—deprivation. That's what it was, sheer, unadulterated deprivation. For two weeks it would be hard-boiled eggs and half a grapefruit twice a day, breakfast and lunch. Dinner was a piece of chicken (not even deep-fried) and a lettuce salad. The grapefruit was supposed to help burn up fat; I have no idea what the egg was supposed to do.

Nothing could stop me now. It's a cinch. Soon I'd be able to stop wearing my father's white shirts over jeans to hide the extra pounds. I'd be just in time for this outcome. My high school was about to put a new dress code in place.

During the grapefruit diet episode I became a hall guard to earn volunteer points, I forget what for. The problem with my slot was that it occurred at the time of one of the lunch periods. I sat in front of the lunch room, and the smell of the fresh french fries was nothing to ignore. I survived the temptation for a few days, but by the end of my second week, I caved. I told myself just a few fries wouldn't hurt. In the end, I gained back whatever weight I had lost with the infamous grapefruit and egg diet, and maybe even put on a bit more.

Later, one of my bosses, who came with a part-time job when I was in art school, suggested I knock off a few pounds.

"You are too cute to be in that body," he said. "Seriously, you should cut out pictures from a beauty magazine, put them on your refrigerator and just as you are ready to eat the ice cream from the freezer look at the images and imagine yourself in their place."

That very night I followed his instructions and even though I considered him a cruel person without any concern for my feelings, I obeyed. I Scotch-taped a picture of a gorgeous red-haired model to my refrigerator. Everything about her was sensational. Her make-up, her dress, her every part was perfection. Every time the fridge door opened I glanced at her and without any remorse, pulled out my favorite ice cream from the freezer, put a few scoops full in a dish and said, "No way."

My final failure at dieting was the jello and cottage cheese diet that I invented. I lasted about two weeks on this concoction. The diet consisted of three meals a day alternating different colors of jello and two textures of cottage cheese for six days, Monday through Saturday. On the seventh day, I rested with a Hershey's chocolate bar.

Finally a light bulb went on. Why did I let myself be bullied into a man's vision of a femme fatale! If and when I was ready, I would be a success. It was all up to me.

So, when my future husband came along I found myself ready all on my own.

A Prompt from Today's Headlines

My father owned a small, low-end furniture and appliance store when I was a young girl. His customers were disadvantaged, low income, working people, struggling to keep their lives together. Dad was understanding of their struggles and decided to sell furniture with a payment plan to all. Without a credit check, he or she was taken at their word and handed a contract with an obligation to pay the company ten dollars a week. Most lived up to the expectation and never cheated. And Dad, who was trusting and caring, never wavered in his kindness and never was disappointed.

He began this way of doing business in the late forties, and continued till 1968, when Martin Luther King, Jr. was killed. Dad's store was ransacked and robbed of $35,000 worth of merchandise. He begged the looters not to burn the store down because in the small apartment above the shop lived a woman who could only get around with a wheelchair. My father was respected and loved by this community located on Kedzie and 16th on Chicago's Westside. And so, because of this connection he had with the people, they listened, and the store was spared.

My concern on that day was of course for my father, who was physically caught in the middle of the fires, the anger, and actions displayed by the rioters. But, on the other hand, I was silently cheering them on because I was outraged and sad that Martin Luther King, Jr., such a wonderful human, was taken down. I had immediately felt their pain and loss of hope for America's future... our future. I witnessed America at its worst. I felt sick and not at all happy with myself because I remembered I had had a chance to cause a riot but it never occurred to me at the time.

In 1962, my husband, who was in the military at that time, and I were stationed at Fort Knox, Kentucky. We had decided to employ a teenager for the summer to help us with our two kids. Melody came from an orphanage in Louisville. She was 16, sweet and somewhat shy. I loved her name, her chocolate brown skin, and the way she had chosen to wear her hair in braids. It was an immediate like. She would stay with us from the end of June until her school resumed in September.

One day, I decided to take a ride with Melody and the kids to Louisville, do some shopping, and have lunch. The city is an hour's drive from Fort Knox. We left about 11 in the morning and on the way, before we got to our destination, the kids got hungry. "We'll eat on the road," I said to Melody, "Look out for some diner."

When we entered the Roadside Eatery, I glanced around to make sure it was clean and had at least some customers occupying the space, just enough to verify its safety. I had no idea about this remote place off the Dixie Highway, the road that led to town. Everything checked out until the manager greeted us with, "Sorry folks there's no available table." That's a lie I thought, I can see about five empty ones which I reported back to the manager.

For about five minutes we argued back and forth. He finally told me I could stand where we were till doomsday, but we would not be served. It didn't make sense to me until Melody tapped my arm and pleaded with me to just leave. I looked at her lovely dark-skinned face and suddenly realized that this guy was a bigot and she knew more about it then I ever could.

Melody was used to this; it was her norm. Her acceptance of his actions made me want to lecture her about fighting back. "It isn't right. Who the hell is he? Let's do something.

We'll call the police." We called nobody, because she wanted to just run away. She wanted out of there!

When we got into the car, the children, five and three, needed some explanation. My almost six-year-old daughter was really into it. It was a good experience for her because it woke her up to the word prejudice. "Remember that word," I told her, "We'll have more conversation about it later."

I have never forgotten this story, and it happened 60 years ago. I regret that I didn't fight hard enough. Bigotry has not changed; it's only gotten worse and America is in shambles, overwhelmed with ignorance.

When I was the child in my parents' home, my father never hesitated to bring his employees home for lunch and sometimes dinner. Never once did he discuss the color of their skin. It wasn't necessary, because my sister and I never gave it a thought other than being excited about COMPANY coming to share a meal. We loved the company.

I still wonder about Melody and if she ever did get to know freedom.

Mother Goose Is On the Loose

My Mother read and reread Mother Goose rhymes to my sister and me so often that they have stayed perfect in my memory. As I became older, I was dumbfounded because my response to the ditties took on a totally different interpretation than I had when I was indulged as a child.

It has occurred to me, the older me, this thought: Why did Humpty Dumpty, such an adorable egg, sit on a wall to begin with? So fragile, so crackable, where was his brain? The truth is he is missing a brain. Eggs don't have brains, they have yolks. Furthermore have you ever tried to put a cracked eggshell together -- imagine horses trying. RIDICULOUS!

As far as the Three Blind Mice running after the farmer's wife just to have their tails cut off? It no longer does it for me. As far as I'm concerned, the farmer's wife needed a lesson on compassion, after all, they were blind. This poem is disabled! I feel guilty that I even listened. And here's a frightening thought, my Mother would end with, "Oh boo-hoo."

And, if there is someone we should worry about, it's Mary who is quite CONTRARY, and so the poem goes on to tell us that next to silver bells and cockleshells she has planted a row of maidens. She dug in the dirt to insert maidens who obliged. What a murderous idea, highly inappropriate to suggest to a child. Supposing the child grows up to be wild---OH MY!

This takes me to the story of "Little Miss Muffet." Why couldn't Miss Muffet just squash the spider? Show some girl power? Men see her running away, and that's what they say and that's what they wrote. Also her choice of food is not so appealing. What kid chooses curds and whey (cottage cheese) for a snack?

Innocent Jack and his girlfriend Jill decided to be helpful. So up the hill they climbed (so far so good), but as fate would have it, their good intentions took a bad turn and Jack fell down and broke his crown and sweet Jill came tumbling after. Moral of the story; no good deed goes unpunished.

One of my favorites is "Sing a Song of Sixpence." Mom sang it to us. Think about it folks, would anyone eat four and twenty blackbirds, baked in a pie? Surely this one needs investigation from the Anti-Cruelty Society. But maybe not, 'cause when the pie was opened the birds began to sing. One even flew away and pecked off the Queen's nose. Maybe what's needed is The Special Victims Unit. Anyway you slice it, it's very interesting -- but stupid!

At first glance "Little Boy Blue" seems like a charming story about a little boy who falls asleep on the job, but upon further investigation, the poem was found to be a protest against a work tax imposed on the poor farmers in the 13th century. Just like politics in all walks of life, it interferes and shows its ugly side.

We all know the tiny house movement, but "There Was an Old Woman Who Lived in a Shoe?" She had so many children she didn't know what to do? The poem expresses poverty, famine and child abuse. Get help, lady, that's what she should do! And some information on birth control wouldn't have hurt.

And so I conclude Mother Goose is something to fear
To fully recover just give me a year.

The Landscape of My Youth

"All the world's a stage, and all the men and women merely players; and one man in his time plays many parts." Shakespeare said that, and lately I keep wanting to go back to where I'm that whining school girl with satchel and shining morning face.

The landscape of my youth has never left me. I close my eyes and see the bungalows and apartment buildings that lined my street. There's my two-flat with a very large tree fully packed with leaves turning bright yellow and red. It's autumn and the beginning of the school year. Maple and oak trees line the streets. Mom, Dad, Sister, Grandma, Grandpa and Uncle Earl fill the apartment. We all lived together for a short period of time during the War. Till this day I love the presence of family, lots of it.

The floor plan was much simpler than the inhabitants. An entrance that handled maybe two people at a time. Soon, quite soon, is the living room and a bedroom on the left of the entrance. A small sunroom follows the living room and surrounding on three sides of the space were windows filled with plants, mostly mother-in-law's tongues. I'm still attached to this succulent. A small entrance, a tiny bathroom, one more bedroom, a dining room, and a kitchen that resembled the one on the set of "The Honeymooners," a TV sitcom in the '50s, completes the place I called home for 16 years.

Grandpa and I sat in the kitchen after my school and his

work day almost every evening through most of the War pulling silver foil off the gum and cigarette wrappers, and pressing the foil into a ball. Once completed, the ball was turned into the factory where my father worked as a War volunteer. From there the foil was put to use making bullets for the soldiers in battle. I looked forward to this activity because Grandpa would use this opportunity to explain every aspect of the battles, and sometimes the news on the radio would fill our time with great details of current affairs. On occasion, my hero, President Roosevelt, would speak to America, but mostly it was Gabriel Heatter and Walter Winchell who gave us the news of the day. I still remember the rhythm of their voices, the seriousness of their words, and Grandpa's words that followed.

"The Hell with you Nazis ---we're gonna get you!"

"Oh, don't tell your mom I used a bad word."

"It's O.K. Grandpa, I'm with you."

Grandpa never got to see the end of the War or his three

sons come home from battle. He died in 1943; the War ended in 1945.

In fall, the trees that lined my street, Springfield Avenue in Chicago, turned the expected colors. Their leaves fell and were then gathered up and made into small bonfires. The roasting smell the flames released was most satisfying. Indescribable! But the most important part of the landscape were the shops I would visit after my school day. Goldie's, a penny candy store, the meat market, the dry goods store named Firebergs, Woolworth's dime store, the first Gonnella Italian bread store with smells that gently rode the winds out the door only to mingle with the Flowers bakery. There was the chicken store that rendered a foul smell, the small 10' by 10' A&P, a pharmacy with a soda bar and cute soda clerk, the first Dominick's grocery, a gift store and a cleaners. Every doorway on the avenue opened up to a proprietor who knew my name, and to this day I can still remember some of theirs.

The walk to school sometimes included conversations with my sister in made-up Italian prompted by a fascination with our neighbors from Italy, and wishing to be part of their world. Seriously made-up gobbly-garbly words blurted out while our hands flew in the air trying to define our meaning. There was no meaning to any of it. We just had fun laughing in make-believe play.

Our favorite room to hang in was the dining room. That's where my sister and I won the War several times while hiding in a tent that we put together with several dining room chairs and a few sheets. We fought hard and managed our wins heroically. This game went on until the end of the War.

My imagination ran wild when I decided that the top of the dining room table would be a stage. My sister and I were sure our performances could be Hollywood masterpieces. Dancing our hearts out with only one capable singer on stage ensured our success. I was told that my voice would ruin our chances, so I only mouthed the words. And of course, there was the proverbial doctor game played on that very stage whenever we were able to get a patient to comply. Once we captured one of the younger boys and dragged him into the apartment with every intention of examining him. When he finally realized what playing doctor meant, he started screaming for his mother. My mother, who was nearby, rescued him and promptly took away my doctor set.

This all was a long time ago, but the memories are still vivid and still bring me joy.

About the Author

For **Trudi Goodman**, writing was always a fun thing to do especially in grade school when at the beginning of every semester the class had to write about their summer vacation.

But the creative possibilities for Trudi were in the visual arts. As a graduate of The Chicago Academy of Fine Arts, she focused on Interior Design and worked in this field for many years. Fine Arts was her passion.

She had many successful years of exhibiting and showing in several galleries in Chicago. Writing memoir reappeared in later life. The two creative processes mirror themselves — and both are a challenge.

Daniel Cleary

Introductory Words

My basic approach to poetry is through song. That's why I rhyme so much. I discovered poetry at a very young age through being part of a verse-speaking choir in school. As I had a stutter, I found speaking syllabically helped me. This has a strong influence on what I write as it helps me when I read it aloud to know where the beats fall in the accented line. There are other approaches to poetry besides this one, of course; poetry doesn't have to rhyme, but I like to think of it as having some inner music if it has to have any lasting attraction for me. The following pieces should be read aloud for full impact.

Ode to Flight (for Steve Fossett)

I

What poet would not envy you!
Slipping the bonds of earth awhile
To sally forth into the blue,
The round earth's bright encircling robe,
And travel on mile after mile
In glorious flight in a balloon
Sustained by your own strength and power,
The winds of chance and good fortune,
To circumnavigate the globe
And be a king of sky and air.

II

I dreamed of such things as a boy
And thought of places I would go
If only I could learn to fly
Or build a plane to lift me up
And let me view the world below
As I afloat upon the breeze
And balancing my tender craft
Would navigate with perfect ease
The atmosphere without mishap
Though half the world might think me daft.

Or sometimes I would dwell for hours
Upon the changes I would make
If only I had superpowers
And could fly anywhere at will;
I'd tear along like some blue streak
Up there among the billowy clouds
And know the freedom flying brings
In its surreal release from crowds
And I would surely know the thrill,
The ecstasy of flying things.

I'd pace along with limber step
As if small wings were at my heels
Or sometimes take a forward leap
As if I could be like Jack Flash;
I used to wonder how it feels
To fly straight upward like a bird
And roam the sky for all to see.
Was there some spell, some magic word
That would enable me to dash
Swiftly between points A & B?

I dreamed long hours without an end.
Who knows the many hours I dreamed?
Every so often I would spend
Entire days thinking how I might
Launch myself out upon the wind.
It seemed an easy thing to do
When it already had been done:
I thought of all the others who
In their own way had dreamed of flight
And had approached it with a run.

A cursory, hop, skip and jump
Before they too like Icarus fell
And hit the ground with a big bump
Their wings all crumpled into bits
A poor, pathetic kite-like shell;
And then one day at Kitty Hawk
Like a miracle it occurred—
Man, who had stood upright to walk
And slowly learned to use his wits
Began to fly, then, like a bird.

Things went much faster after that.
Development was swift and sure.
Improvements followed fast on what
Had fascinated from the start
And always had a great allure.
Soon planes were flying everywhere
Until today they span the skies
And dominate the light blue air
In ways no bike, no horse or cart
Could ever hope to equalize.

Yet somehow in some way we lost
That first connection that we had
With what we always prized the most—
The simple, natural urge to fly,
To rise above, to be made glad,
To move about both up and down
Or to move forward as one wished,
To travel to another town,
To skirt the clouds above, to hie
O'er hill and dale and not feel rushed.

Pure flight to me is wind alone
Is piloting a flimsy craft
Somehow or other on your own
Into some new strange element
That lifts it with a certain heft
And sets it on a steady course.
It's floating silently as fluff
Without a great degree of force
Or consequent rough sediment
That comes from oil and other stuff.

Pure flight is what it was back then
And what you gallantly portrayed
In five attempts before this one;
Something that's individual
And has the air of being homemade;
Something that's highly dangerous
And takes a large degree of trust
— Braving the high winds pitch and toss —
And an indomitable will
That you won't end up being lost.

III

Heading due east into the sun
You set out on that windswept day,
Your marvelous journey had begun.
A sweet elation filled your breast
Now you were clear and on your way.
You rose up in the surging drafts
The bouncing currents of your dream
Like feather down that softly wafts
Itself aloft when slightly pressed
And latches on to the airstream.

Daniel Cleary

You shot along at a brisk pace,
The currents of the air were fleet
Soon you had passed the very place
Where you had faltered once before
And came close almost to defeat.
The silent heavens took you in,
They wrapped you round and held you close;
At night you felt freed from the din,
Out on a sea without a shore,
Of what would bother your repose.

And then--- was it in Kalgoorlie
In Australia, you set down?
I'm sure it's true, it's not a lie!
Having gone clear around the world
You landed near this little town.
What did you tell them of your trip
That seemed touched with the fabulous,
Once you had got them in your grip
As they listened to your tale unfold
Circled around you in the grass?

The Queen's Hats

Today I'm going to talk about the Queen's hats
Which come in various shapes and sizes
And act almost like an alternate crown.
Amazing, when you think of it--
The lady herself is quite diminutive
Which is a curious anomaly
Because she wields such immense power--
For all that she is extraordinarily dignified.
But getting back to her hats.
You have to be curious as to who it is
Makes them, and how it comes about
She picks and chooses them?
I have to admit I'm inclined
To have a great affection for the Queen
Even though, as an Irishman
And the son of an ardent Republican,
You have to wonder what that makes me.
Totally lost, perhaps.
Anyway, as I was saying, her hats…
Now and then she does wear a crown
On special State Occasions
And when she does looks even more magnificent.

At the Pictures

Tony Curtis in *The Prince Who Was a Thief*
Or Jeff Chandler in *Flame of Araby*
Whatever it was, movies brought the whole world to us
On those Saturday afternoons in the early fifties:
Once I remember seeing *Pagan Love Song*
With a hoard of screaming kids like myself.
But the quieter moments I remember too
Those first intimations of love when the hero
Swept the girl up into his arms and kissed her
Or when the director and cinematographer,
Not to say the composer of the musical score,
And the actors themselves, managed to carry through to me
Profundities I could not yet put a name on.
So, it was we became acquainted with shadows and fog,
With secret assignations and baffling intrigues,
With trench-coated spies and dazzling blondes,
With night train journeys and city streets.
Films like *Where the Sidewalk Ends, The Big Clock,*
This Gun for Hire or *The Asphalt Jungle*
All that detritus of the Second World War
Lingered over us and shed its influence on us.
Then, of course, there were the lighter moments:
The comedies, and let's not forget, the Hollywood musicals.
Those great big M.G.M. blockbusters
That filled our souls with the quintessence of romance:

And Then We Wrote

Gene Kelly, Judy Garland, Fred Astaire,
Singing in the Rain and *Easter Parade*
And the westerns --I haven't even mentioned the westerns!

In that small town close to the Galtee Mountains
It was hard to know where the real world ended
And the imaginary world began.
There was such a swift interchange between them.
Even the theatres, the Excel and, the Gaiety
Were designed with Hollywood, California in mind
So immediately on entering you felt
You had just stepped into a large mansion in Beverly Hills
Replete with fountains and all kinds of extravagances:
Full length mirrors and pools where fishes swam.
It was my later good fortune to work in both these theaters
As a projectionist, starting at the age of sixteen.
So it was, my education became complete
And I became marked for life as an otherworldly dreamer.

A Selection of Sonnets

On Seeing a Photo of Greta Garbo (for Elena)

Who has looked at the depthless gaze of love
Or known, for one brief moment out of time,
Exactly what it is it takes to move
A vagrant spirit's venture into rhyme--
Numbering, for a humbler clientele,
What's often only guessed at secondhand
Endeavoring while underneath its spell
To make it clear, that all might understand.
Such sober beauty is a case in point.
Impervious to the battering of the waves
Around its base, it rises to anoint
Another generation, calmly saves
What else might be dispersed with, known for naught:
What countless men have worshipped, vainly sought.

On Hearing Birdsong After a Thunderstorm

I wake and listen, such ecstatic spirit
Raises to the sky its tremulous song
In tuneful caroling, though not for long—

It's over, almost before I think of it.

And then another bird goes tweet-tweet-tweet
As if in answer; coming right along
To soon be followed by a garrulous throng
Lending support in chorus bit by bit.

An ordinary day, unhallowed from the start,
Finding us glum and heavy in our shoes;
Who would have thought it might take such a turn?

And not too long, after the morning news
And diverse ills—more than can be discerned—
Its sheer audacity restores my spirit.

Laundry

We waken to the world of laundry.
Flapping bedsheets and flying pillowcases
Compete with the fluttering of lively shirttails
To help us see the positive side of things.
The spirit rises within us in thankfulness.
What, after all, are better than beginnings
Even if they are, in some measure, only illusory?
Monday morning brings its own considerations:
The start of a new week, the unfolding
Over time of what may soon be revealed to us--
Whether it turns out to be for good or ill
Is hardly important-- That we are here, now,
And the brave scent of laundry enlivens our senses
Promises nothing but good days ahead.

Daniel Cleary

How to Write a Sonnet

Always from sure beginnings make a start
No matter if you don't know where to go;
Follow what might be truly called your heart
But keep the old brain ticking even so.

Allow for some discursions on the way,
Some commentaries and other brief asides,
Remember, though, for all you have to say,
Your movements are still governed like the tides.

Be careless, carefree, even for all that
No matter if, wherever 'tis you're bound
You wind up there at last without your hat
Your two feet, somehow, having left the ground.

Discoursing wildly on, of all things, love,
Like nothing else on earth or heaven above.

Something New

Something new – bright of wing
Something new – today I sing
Something new – to show the way
Point us to a better day
A way out of this impasse
We've got ourselves into, alas.

Something new – a symphony
Full of colors we can see
A whole new bright array of words
Backed by a brand-new set of chords
To raise us up, to make a stand
Form ourselves into a band.

Something new – in these dire times
A melody affixed with rhymes
We will not very soon forget
To help unite us, once more set
Our thoughts upon a higher plane
That we might find our way again.

Daniel Cleary

I'm Off, Good Day!

Ranged like battalions in the grass,
Scattered all around en masse,
I see below me as I pass
Armies of flowers.

Above me in the blue, blue sky,
Gloriously grand and high,
I see slowly passing by
A few stray clouds.

This morning in my sunlit walk
There's nobody with whom to talk
The bird is busy on the stalk
And I'm away.

Who'll miss me for the next few hours,
Which promise to be free of showers,
Or even bother? By the powers,
I'm off, good day!

About the Author

Daniel Cleary is a painter as well as a poet. He has published four books of poetry. They are: *The Green Ribbon*. Enright House of Ireland, 1991; *Elegy for James Gerard and Other Poems for the Larger Voice*. Fractal Edge Press, 2004; *A Few Stray Leaves*. Lagoons Editions, 2015; and, *Wave* (First edition). Lagoons Editions, 2019.

Ann Fiegen

Introductory Words

During this year, more than ever before, writing is for me cathartic. Putting pen to paper is one thing that has not been denied, one thing I can do for myself, and hopefully for the enjoyment of others. I am most comfortable writing memoir, but have found that the poetic form provides yet another genre to use in telling my stories. I have enjoyed experimenting in telling the same story in both memoir and poetic genres as well as in writing freestanding poems.

We Three

In the early sixties, we sat together in the student union, smoked our Marlboros, and discussed many things — our classes, our boyfriends, our futures. Still in our teens, our giggles were girlish, our dreams abundant, our idealism intact. When Kennedy was shot, we huddled together, not knowing what to do. The world changed on that day, and we, too, were forever changed - dramatically diminished by our country's loss of innocence.

We graduated, became engaged, married and had babies. We witnessed the Women's Movement, freed our breasts from restrictive bras and wore t-shirts saying things like *A Woman Needs a Man Like a Fish Needs a Bicycle*. We met for meals, for play dates (although we never used that silly nomenclature), and we spoke of our careers (or lacks thereof), our husbands, our babies. Many times we helped one another hold it all together in our new roles as wives and mothers. Still in our twenties, we found ourselves playing very adult roles. The transition from our recent girlhoods was not easy, but we were in it together, and we got through it together with laughter and tears. One year at a time, we moved through our lives, never losing touch, never moving far away, the three of us, forever friends, soul sisters.

And now, we're here, in our *Golden Years*. Even typing the term makes me laugh. Having to be old together is an entirely new experience, and not particularly golden in nature. We often look at one another and ask how the F%#@ did we get this old? It is a constant source of amazement, and poses a question for which there is no answer. It happens to everyone, but somehow we thought it would never happen to us, but believe it or not, like it or not, we're old. Luckily we get to be old together.

Our conversations involve a lot of health talk.

Have you had the new shingles shot? How's your cholesterol? Blood pressure? Bone density? Seeing better now that you've had your cataracts taken care of? How's Ken doing on that dementia medication? And Patrick, are his speech issues connected to his Parkinson's?

It goes on and on, never even getting close to anything golden.

Collectively we have a good memory, individually not so much. Conversations often go like this:

I saw a good movie last week.
What was it?
I can't remember the name, but it starred
that guy that was married to ... the woman who
was in that movie about depression.

or

You know, I've been thinking a lot lately about...
Oh my God, I forgot what I was going to say.

Golden? I don't think so.

But then there's the laughter, the really good kind that hurts your belly and makes you cry. We've been laughing like that together for decades, and now that we're old, there's so much more to laugh about. So, once we've moved through the health talk and the memory gap pauses, we get to the funny times. There are so many stories, so many hilarious experiences we have shared that never cease to make us laugh. And that laughter makes the being old stuff all worthwhile. The ability to laugh knows no age limits. It's not something we used to do but can't now because we're too old, like playing tennis or pulling an all-nighter. It is soul satisfying and restorative. It separates us from the beasts, and does more for our serotonin uptake than any anti-anxiety medication. It is all this and more, and no one laughs harder than we three when we're together.

Supportive and sustaining, deep and devoted, tried and true, ours is the friendship of a lifetime. Pretty golden after all.

We Three

We three were there
In the student union
Smoking our Marlboros
Discussing many things
Boyfriends   classes   final exams
Movies   music   life
Impossibly young
All hopes and dreams

We three were there
On that November day
When Oswald's shots
Shattered innocence
Changing all we knew
Kennedy died on that day
Life as we knew it
Died too

Ann Fiegen

We three were there
Through the years that followed
With breakneck speed
Mini skirts   go-go boots   discotechs
Weddings   babies   careers
Our 20s 30s 40s and on
Matrimony   motherhood   middle age menopause
And now

We three are here
The Golden Years
Meeting for a meal
Laughing with abandon
At all we have shared
And sometimes simultaneously
Crying without reservation
At what we have lost

We three are here
Knowing just how to be
With one another
No questions asked
Time after time year after year
Joined at our souls
No one could be closer
Than we three

The Things We Keep

For reasons known only to her, my mother kept an inordinate amount of my baby things. Traveling with us in every move, were boxes containing my baby clothes, little golden books, teething rings, rattles and baby toys. On a larger scale, there was my baby carriage, my disassembled wooden playpen and my highchair. I must admit, I never thought much about it, but in retrospect, it was more than a little strange.

There was a time, however, when I saw some benefit to her having kept so much and for so long. I was expecting my first child, and money was tight. During a visit to my mother's house, I spotted that old high chair in the basement. It definitely looked old, and a little rough around the edges, but it would be fine, and the price was right. So I took it home, cleaned it up, painted it yellow, and deposited it in a prominent place in the kitchen to await future use.

And it had a lot of use. Eventually all three of my sons sat their chubby legs in it for every meal until they were big enough to sit in a regular chair. The chair served us well for years, and then, when the last boy moved to his big boy chair, it went to the garage, where it stayed until we moved. In that move, and in every one that followed, it went with us. Three times I consciously decided to bring it along, and then following our divorce, I took custody and chose to keep it with me the four times when I moved alone.

Last Friday was big trash pick up day in Evanston, one of

the two times a year residents can get rid of their big *stuff* for free. I had a relatively long list of items I needed to get rid of, and my youngest son came to help me haul things out. One by one, we went through the garage, the pile in the alley increasing by leaps and bounds. There were boxes of once treasured cookbooks that no one wants or needs. Bye, bye, Julia Child and company. Boxes of video and audio tapes, a bright red Adirondack chair made for me by my oldest son, but having fallen victim to rot, an old compost bin, a metal shelving unit, the pile kept growing. At last, after what seemed a very long time, we came to the end.

It was then that I stood in front of the yellow highchair. I consciously thought about the fact that it had been with me for my entire life. I saw the faces of my babies sitting in it, and recalled that I had painted over a teddy bear decal that was on the back of the seat. I acknowledged that there was a way in which I loved that chair, but the time had come to put it out with the trash. It was a chair, for God's sake. No one wants it. Time to get rid of it.

Put this one out there, too. I can't watch you do it,
but I'll go in the yard while you put it out.

And then the tears started, coming from a place in my soul so deep that I didn't know it was there. I cried because to me it was more than a chair. It was a presence, a presence with me throughout all my life, a link, if you will, to all that had passed, a constant amid all of life's changes.

Mom, just keep it. It doesn't take up any room, just keep it.

And so I did. I kept it, and today I cleaned it up and brought it into the house where occasionally I can see it and know that it is there because I want it to be, because I need it to be. Some things you just need to keep, and there's nothing strange about it.

Legacy

My father so seldom present
Focused or sober
Disappointed so many times
Those disappointments were the bricks
Of the wall I built around me
To keep me safe

When he died I could see no place
Where he had ever been

With time
My wall of bricks
Has cracked
Allowing me to see
Bits of his legacy
Small proofs that he once was here

That place I couldn't find
Is there now

Ann Fiegen

In the blue of my middle son's eyes
The strong, square hands of my youngest
There in the athletic prowess
Of my grandson
By far always
The best player on his team

Now when I sleep
The wall is gone

In my dreams
He comes back
He is close to me
Close enough
To find his place
In my heart

Reunion

For me, one of the great things about being a kid was that it took me a long time to realize exactly how dysfunctional my family really was. I spent a good portion of my childhood in blissful ignorance, not once considering the fact that maybe, just maybe, my family unit was about as far from mainstream as it could be. There was my long suffering mother for whom nothing and no one was ever enough, my alcoholic father for whom booze was always the answer no matter the question, and me, their only child, who more often than not found herself playing the role of parent. And then there was my maternal grandmother. Let's get it straight from the get-go, Anna was not in any way your traditional grandmother, you know, the one in the Hallmark commercials who greets her family at Thanksgiving in her house full of delicious fragrances and hand-knit afghans.

Because she lived with us for 12 years, her presence was a constant in my childhood. She occupied the second bedroom of our two-bedroom walk-up above a drug store on Chicago's west side. Her room is permanently etched in my mind. It was always dark in there, and it usually smelled of a combination of orange peels and a brand of bath soap called Sweetheart, which, rather than smelling clean, smelled sickeningly sweet. While not totally unpleasant, the smell sometimes made me want to gag. To this day I have a problem with the smell of orange peels.

In one corner of the room, next to the often-hissing radiator, stood her right leg. It was an actual artificial appendage made out of wood complete with a wooden foot, knee joint, and sturdy fabric straps with metal buckles to attach it to her body. There was always a black, old lady tie shoe on that foot. She had been in her early sixties when the gangrenous infection in her foot required that her leg be amputated just above the knee. Because of the cumbersome nature of the primitive prosthetic, she never really learned to navigate efficiently with it, so more often than not, it stood in that corner. Actually, it *loomed* in that corner, like another presence in the room. There was a bed there, never made, a small dresser, and a lamp featuring an old-fashioned girl in a pink dress holding a basket of flowers.

Her still-auburn hair was always secured into a kind of bun. A freestanding radio stood on her left, and crutches on her right. Because she had cataracts, she wore thick-lensed glasses that were usually all smudged up, making her already impaired vision even worse.

The child that I was viewed her certainly as an oddity and, at times, as an embarrassment. When I became old enough to have friends over after school, I remember hoping she wouldn't appear so I could avoid answering the myriad questions that would certainly be posed.

Who is that?
  My grandmother.
What happened to her other leg?
  They had to take it off.
Why?
  Because it got infected.
Can she see?
  A little.
Is she mean?
  Not really.

I don't recall ever spending much time with her, nor her

ever requesting that I do. We lived out our years together without ever touching on any level, or even ever trying to. I was an adult when she died, and didn't know her any better than when I was a child. I'm sorry to say I never asked her questions that would have allowed me to know more of the woman she was. Why did she come to America? As a divorced single mother at a time when that was an oddity, how did she support herself and her children? Did she have a great love in her life? What were her dreams? So many questions I failed to ask, so many answers I will never know.

She once told me that her father had the job of putting bells in the highest steeples in Prague. There is a blue and white bowl that now sits in my kitchen counter that she said was the only piece she had taken with her when she immigrated to the United States. I have a small, lined notebook dated 1907, containing love poems written in pencil in her unmistakable hand. Her favorite song was *In the Shade of the Old Apple Tree*, and her favorite meal was pork chops, dumplings and sauerkraut. That's it, all I know of her or have left of her life.

I feel a lot of regret that I don't know more, that I allowed our lives to be parallel and missed any connection that we might have had. Because we were so closely related, I'm sure there are ways in which we are alike, and I take responsibility for not having taken the time to identify and perhaps even nurture those likenesses. I definitely missed what might have been an important connection.

Some years ago, I was lucky enough to visit Prague. Because that lovely city is a sea of antiquities, it was easy for me to imagine her there, walking as I did down cobbled streets, stopping perhaps for a coffee and kolache along the way. I heard her voice in the rhythm of the language spoken by the locals and imagined how her reflection as a young woman might have looked in the windows of the shops as I passed.

It was an unexpectedly emotional time for me. I barely knew this woman who was my grandmother, yet I could feel her presence with me as I explored the city of her birth. I felt a connection with her there that I never once experienced during our time together. Curiously, although my sense of direction is so poor that I frequently lose my way in my own neighborhood, I never once got lost in Prague. And, one time while hurrying down a crowded street, I heard a little voice in my head telling me to look down. When I did, I saw a hand reaching for my purse. I yelled, the robber ran, and my purse remained in my possession. Coincidences? Maybe.

On my last day in Prague, I went for a walk by myself. I came to a church where the sounds of an organ drifted out of the open doors. Taking that as an invitation, I went inside and sat for a long time in a pew in the back, hypnotized by the music that surrounded me. It was a pipe organ, and because of the vibrations it created in that relatively confined space, I could actually feel the music course through my body.

When it stopped, and the surprisingly young organist left the building, I tried to stay for a while longer in that place where his music had taken me, but after a few minutes, I left my seat and returned to the street outside. At the precise moment I stepped out of the doors, the sound of church bells rang out not just from that church, but also from churches throughout the city. I looked up and around and could see many of the highest steeples in Prague, their bells triumphantly ringing in unison.

Hi, Gram, good to be with you.

April 19th

The psychics call them visitation dreams. They are the dreams we have about those we love after they die. There is a list of criteria to determine if your dream about your departed loved one qualifies, a kind of step-by-step guide to establish its authenticity. For example, it has to seem incredibly real, so real that when you wake up you are convinced it really happened. The departed has to appear vibrant and healthy, they don't engage in idle chit chat, but rather come with a purpose. Although I have had many dreams about people whom I loved after they died, I have never thought for a moment that they were anything more than just dreams. Never, that is, until last night.

He was at first, in the background. I could see him, but there were several people between us. He stood still, and I moved toward him one person at a time. He was wearing that favorite blue blazer that needed to be replaced, a white button-down shirt and the striped grey silk tie I bought for him in Paris. There was a spot on the tie. There was always a spot on his tie. His hair was still wet from his shower and curling up in the back, and there was a little razor nick near the cleft in his chin. He opened his arms, I took one step forward, and there it was, that feeling again of his arms around me, the smell of his shampoo, the absolute contentment I always found up in his embrace.

What are you doing here?
It's my birthday.

And then I was awake. Wide awake. It was still dark in my room, and I was still alone in my bed, but there had been a reconnection. For a brief moment he had been with me, so acutely, so vividly, that I had a hard time convincing myself that it was a dream.

It may very well be that the entire experience was brought about by a combination of things, the fact that today is his birthday, the tenth since he died, the COVID social distancing that has rendered hugs the most precious of commodities, the fact that I met with his kids and grandkids on Zoom last week. Who knows? And, I guess, who cares?

What I do know for sure is that Cinderella was right, *A dream is a wish your heart makes when you're fast asleep.*

April 19th

My closed eyes see him clearly
Well-worn jacket
Shaving nick on his chin
Spot on my favorite tie

He stands still
I move toward him
Dodging those
Between us

I'm there
His arms hold me
Familiar   safe
Like it used to be

Happy Birthday whispered
Into his chest
Then again
Happy Birthday

Ann Fiegen

Too soon
I open my eyes
He's gone
I'm
Alone

Happy Birthday

At the Lake

In times like these
With so much different
Our lives altered
Our futures unsure
The Lake is
My place that is
The same

The sun still rises over the water
Waves still caress the shore
Just as all those years ago
When I became engaged there
Then brought my boys there
To swim and play
And get browned by the sun

The Harbor is the same
Moored boats ready to sail
The Bahá'í keeping watch
With quiet elegance
Over all who pass
Over all who linger
To absorb the peace

Ann Fiegen

It is there I go
Seeking sameness
To remember
To forget
To be me again
To feel a part of
Rather than distant from

Duck families join me there
For the peanuts I bring
And today a chipmunk
Ate from my hand
Sharing a moment
Of trust
And union

A sweet reminder
That these small moments
Are special gifts
That need to be savored
Precious treasures
That help keep us hopeful
In times like these

About the Author

Ann Fiegen is a joyously retired mother and grandmother for whom part of the joy comes from her being able to spend less time doing what she has to and more doing what she wants to. She reads, gardens, watches birds through binoculars, feeds the chipmunks from her hand, spends every chance she can get with her grandchildren, enjoys time with other ladies who lunch, and last but not least, to satisfy her soul, she writes.

Fumiko Tokunaga Jensen

Introductory Words

When I was a young child in Japan, I loved books and preferred reading more than playing outside. I dreamed about writing books and poems when I grew up. But somehow I went in a different direction, becoming a musician, and continued my whole life as a professional musician. But when I retired, I wanted to realize my childhood dream. Living in a foreign country, it was not easy writing in my third language (my second language is Danish). But I keep on writing even while feeling awkward about my imperfect English.

New York Story I

Watching CNN, Anderson Cooper was saying, besides New York, New Jersey's coronavirus cases have increased too. I was lying down in front of the TV with my sleepy brain, recovering from more than a whole month-long flu or whatever I had. Some people suggested "depression?" Maybe, but I have no reason to get depressed. My daughter says "probably the weather?" That is more likely. It's almost in the middle of April and the trees are still dry and no flowers, even no buds, no sunshine, sometimes cold winds. It's depressing.

So I was lying down on the floor like a mollusk, half asleep. But the words New Jersey suddenly woke my memory up. I could see myself standing on a desolate country road in somewhere, New Jersey, waiting for a bus which I don't know was coming or not. It's getting darker and back then not only New York but New Jersey as well were dangerous. I came on time for the bus schedule but you can't trust the schedule at all, sometimes I had to wait for one hour. Summer was sort of OK, but winter was cold and dark. After about a 45-minute bus ride on a dark road, suddenly the luminous top of the Empire State Building appears, and while you are watching with wonder, the whole view of glittering Manhattan appears. This was the highlight of my lonely weekly travel to New Jersey. When the bus crossed to Manhattan, Port Authority was right there and our apartment was next to the building.

We lived in a luxury apartment on 42nd St. between 9th

and 10th Aves, Manhattan. It was built for some wealthy people obviously, but the location was too dangerous; no one would buy it. Then the government bought it and started renting it out to poor artists for very reasonable rent, just $250 per month for two full-size bedrooms with two bathrooms and a big bathtub.

We didn't have any furniture of course. We bought two mattresses and slept on the floor. There was a secondhand store nearby, where we bought plates and pots and pans. One day, my husband came back from the East Side with a beautiful, black reclining chair which he found on the street. Ever since that day, he went to the East Side every Wednesday, because Wednesday was the day people on the East Side put their furniture on the street. My cellist husband was freelancing, but was far from making a living, so I went to Westchester and New Jersey, I've forgotten the name of the city, to teach piano and on Saturdays, I taught in a Japanese school in Newark. This was safe travel, just take a subway to George Washington Bridge then change to a bus to Newark to a school. I taught 1st graders, all Japanese children, and I fell in love with all of them.

New York Story 2

Hans was carrying a cello and I, a footstool, in West Village, New York. In front of a bookstore, I stopped and told him "Here" and put down the stool. But he was not sure, hesitatingly saying, " I don't want to do it." Then I said firmly "It's your idea. Do it!" After a couple of minutes, he reluctantly opened the cello case, sat down on the stool and started tuning the cello. Prelude from Bach's D minor solo cello sonata started quietly streaming on the street.

I was standing in front, pretending to be an audience and even put money in the cello case which was laid open in front of him. When the Prelude was finished, I applauded loudly. In the beginning, no one was stopping but after a while, one after another started to stop and listened and started filling up money in the cello case, though one person picked a couple of bills from the case to put them in his pocket and ran away.

We lived in a three-bedroom apartment in the Upper East Side with two roommates plus one of the roommate's father who was sleeping on our living room sofa. He escaped from Romania to count on his supposed-to-be-a-successful-businessman son. The son and the father both wore pinstripe suits everyday, looking like perfectly dressed businessmen, but when they wanted to pick up suits from a laundry store, often they didn't have enough money. I remember they were counting all money from pockets including coins and sometimes they had to wait to pick up the suits. The son was a very good cook too. When Hans had played a cello concerto with the Juilliard School orchestra at Alice Tully Hall, he cooked elaborate food for the after-concert party.

We had another roommate, a medical student from Israel, who sold arts posters to make extra money. One day in the beginning of May, when most of our friends went home for the summer vacation, our roommates and we did not have enough money to travel. The roommate from Israel and his girlfriend had suggested we should go to Cape Cod. Then we all started to think how to make money for the coming vacation.

Hans's street musician job went very well. The end of the day, counting money, mostly coins, was the best part of the day. But the summer progressed and lots of tourists were coming to the Village, the street started filling up with many street artists with loud pop music and no one was able to listen to quiet Bach. After our roommate's suggestion, Hans had changed the location. In front of the Metropolitan Museum, below the stairs, and I sold posters, which our roommate lent to me.

The business was very successful until one day a magician with a black cape with a big black magician hat appeared and started a magic show and all the audience went to see his magic. Hans was left alone playing quiet Bach. Competitive Hans was very upset saying, "Well, I can do it too."

Back in the Village, this time he didn't play cello, but was doing a magic show. Quickly, a big crowd surrounded him, and they were applauding and laughing. The show was seemingly successful, but when I walked around with a hat to collect money, people left without paying anything.

By the end of the summer, we had saved enough money to rent a car and drove up to Cape Cod. While we were riding rented bicycles in the fresh summer breeze on the island, I shouted to Hans with a big smile, "So beautiful! Isn't it great?"

New York Story 3

One afternoon, Hans said he is very tired and has a terrible headache. We were supposed to play a debut recital that evening in Carnegie Recital Hall that is called nowadays Weill Recital Hall, a small hall next to big Carnegie Hall.

Helmut, our roommate from Switzerland, and I didn't take it seriously. Both of us said "Oh, it's normal when you are worried and nervous for tonight's performance." I could see Hans was trying to convince himself. "Yes, it must be nervousness."

The recital started in the evening. Normally, we stream our musical thoughts to each other, back and forth until they start flowing together and become one river which we send to the audience. But that evening, I kept sending musical thought to him but nothing came back. He has always been a passionate, strong musician and usually I am the one who supports and helps him express his musical expression. But that whole evening, nothing developed musically. The end of the evening, I had unsatisfactory, empty feelings.

When we went back to our Upper West Side apartment where friends were preparing an after-concert party, Hans didn't look good, pale and very tired, hugely different from his normal self, none of his usual silly jokes. When I took his temperature with a thermometer, he had a very high temperature, almost 105 degrees. He had the flu.

Fortunately, we had several concerts in Weill Recital Hall and other venues in New York City later, which all went very

well. But this debut concert was the worst memory of Hans'
musical career.

New York Story 4

It was May 1979 at Juilliard School of Music's final test performance right before summer vacation. I had just finished accompanying Hans on the piano and came out from the room where the test occurred. Another cello student was waiting for her turn to perform and she asked me to accompany her because her pianist didn't show up for some reason. I agreed and played with her.

After the performance, she invited Hans and me for tea at her apartment at 72nd Street and Central Park West. When we arrived at her building, the first thing I noticed was the most extraordinarily elegant elevator I had ever seen in my life. The elevator had dark wooden paneled walls, a bench, and a carved lion head. Inside the apartment was also luxuriously furnished. We were dumbfounded looking around and seeing that she was living in such luxury.

When she invited us to one of the bedrooms, a young girl, maybe around 9 years old, was sitting on a bed with curtains and an expensive looking bedcover. With her beautiful dress and gracious behavior, she looked like a princess. We were even more puzzled thinking who is she? Younger sister? Then the young woman explained to us that she was a live-in babysitter for this child. Finally we grasped the whole situation.

She told us that the building is called The Dakota and many famous people were living in this building, like New

York Philharmonic's legendary conductor, Leonard Bernstein, Yoko Ono, John Lennon and many other famous people.

Soon after, we heard the news that John Lennon was killed in the entrance of this building.

New York Story 5

International House was on Claremont Avenue and 123rd Street, Manhattan, almost Harlem. Columbia University was nearby. Lots of young people from all over the world who came to study in New York were staying there. A married couple like us were not allowed to stay, but there were a couple of music rooms with a grand piano in the basement where I could practice. So I went there every day to practice. I got to know so many people from different countries there, who became lifelong friends.

But after some years of young free life, in Manhattan, I got pregnant. We had no income or health insurance. My mother wanted me to come to Japan for delivering the baby. But my husband had several concert engagements in Denmark when I was due and he wanted to be there when the baby is coming. So we decided, I'll go to Denmark.

While I still was in the hospital with our newborn son, my husband got an offer for the principal cello position in Denmark's best orchestra. His parents were so happy and my mother whom I called in Japan to tell the good news, was so relieved, her voice was ecstatic.

One day, one week after I and the baby came out from the hospital, my husband and I were walking in the countryside near my in-laws' house with the baby in a baby carriage. None of us were talking. We were in deep silence. Suddenly, both of us stopped walking and looked at each other. He said, "Let's go back to New York!"

I said immediately, "Yes!!" People may not understand why we will leave the secure job and go back to uncertainty in dangerous New York, but we both felt staying here in peaceful Denmark means the end of our youth and sounded boring.

Back in New York, by pure luck, we were allowed to live in a great, government-owned apartment building for poor artists. But I couldn't travel to International House for practicing piano several hours everyday because of the baby.

Some friends told us one could buy a piano with little money in one place in Brooklyn. We went to the piano shop in Brooklyn with the baby in a snuggly.

It was a shabby store; you can't even call it a store. The small room was filled with only two baby grands. But one of them was not bad at all, not great but useable and the price was incredibly low, $1500. But for us, it was lots of money. After some negotiations, the owner agreed to go down to $1000. But I knew all we had in our bank was around $1000 or less. My husband is not a good negotiator and I am not either. But in this situation, someone has to be tough. So I suggested $700.

Of course, he said "No." Then I said, "Ok, that's fine, we don't want it then," and started walking away with the baby in my snuggly. Then the man said, "OK, OK, Fine! $700!"

When we came back to Manhattan, it was already dark. We got a piano but how long can we survive with so little money? We went to a nearby ATM machine to check how much money was left or even worse, nothing left?

To our surprise, there was $2000 in the bank. I cried and knew it was my mother who had sent it.

Mother's intuition is always incredible. Also to become a mother made me strong.

My Mother's Cooking

I wish I could write about my mother's cooking like people often talk about with nostalgic childhood memories. I have none of them because I never had a chance to try it. She never cooked. I wish she had. I wish she taught me how to cook. As a result, I had a hard time with cooking and other housework later in my life. This sounds like I had a bad mother. In a way she was for failing to teach me the practical everyday chores. But I loved her anyway, and she loved me dearly.

She was a professional haiku poet. She often worked the whole night when it was close to the deadline for the haiku magazine for which she wrote. Before she sent the haiku to the editor, she let me choose the best ones even though I was the youngest in the family, at 12 or 13 years old. Maybe because I was a bookworm. I remember how proud I was.

She was a free-thinker, not a conventional mother, which was rare among Japanese women in her generation. Fortunately we had a housekeeper who cooked and did all the housework. She often asked me what I'd like for dinner and often made my favorite dishes. She was like my second mother.

Before my mother passed away, I went to Japan because I was informed by my sisters that her memory was slipping away. When I saw her, she said, "Oh Sugako, so nice to see you." Sugako was the wife of one of my cousins. Even though I was prepared, I was so shocked. I could not say a word and started to cry. Then she looked worried and tried to console me saying, "Dear Sugako, I am so sorry to see you so sad. What happened?" Still I couldn't say a word and started to cry more intensely.

At night, someone had to sleep next to her because she could fall when she tried to go to the bathroom in the middle of the night. Lying next to her in the dark bedroom, I said to her, "When I could not fall asleep as a child, I often slipped into your bed. Do you remember?" To my surprise, she said, "Of course I do," with a smiling voice. And she continued our conversations with the things she regretted in her life with a remorseful voice. But the next morning, she slipped away again and could not recognize me.

I had to go back to Chicago after a week since my children were waiting for me. Soon after, she passed away. My consolation was the memory of my conversation with her that night.

Buddha's Wife

When I was growing up in Japan, I never thought about Buddhism or any religion for that matter. Later in my life when I took interest in the philosophy of Buddhism, I realized how much everyday life and even language in Japan is interconnected with Buddhism.

New Year's Eve is my most significant childhood memory related to Buddhism. I used to fall asleep listening to the distant tolling of a temple bell. The bell gonged 108 times, once for each of the vices that cause sufferings to humans. Occasionally we went to a ceremony at a Buddhist temple for the death of a relative or acquaintance. Sitting properly with our legs folded under us in the Japanese fashion for a long time listening to a sutra chanted by a monk and not understanding a word, was especially difficult as children. The big room was unbearably cold in winter and humid in the summer, the chanting mixed up with a continuous chorus of cicadas made us sleepy. When we were finally allowed to stand up, our legs were so numb we were not able to stand on our feet.

As I grew older, living far away from Japan, even though I do not consider myself religious, I often found the teaching and philosophy of Buddhism helpful when going through hardships in life.

I recently became reacquainted with one story about the Buddha that I had heard long ago. The story was about Siddhartha Gautama, a prince in a small kingdom in India, who left his young wife and newborn baby when he was 29 years old.

Ever since first hearing this story, my reaction was: What a cruel thing to do to his family. How did his wife handle the situation? She must have felt abandoned and asked herself, "Did he ever love me? What about our baby? How can I live from now on?" For all these years since initially hearing the story, I tried not to think about this historical fact because it did not seem to fit the core teaching of Buddhism: "Benevolence."

This summer, I found a book in which the author wrote about this same story. He wrote that later in her life Buddha's wife, Yaśodharā, became one of Buddha's disciples and so did the child he left behind, when he grew up. Reading this already began to ease my mind about the story. The author continued that he has been thinking about this story for many years. He had also imagined how Yaśodharā must have felt.

Their wedding day was perhaps the first time they met each other. The teenage Yaśodharā must have thought, that noble, beautiful prince was different from all the other young men she had met before. When they started their life together, she observed carefully this young, quiet husband who was melancholic and often deep in thought. As she grew from a young bride into an older, mature woman, she developed a deep understanding of him. Yaśodharā thought to herself, "He is not an ordinary man. He seems distressed by something very important. He is concerned about his fellow human beings and the world. That must be the matter of his concern. It is not because he doesn't love his family, but it is crucial for him to start a long journey to solve the problem. One day he will leave us to search for truth. I must prepare myself for that day."

That day arrived and Siddhartha told Yaśodharā, "In this distressed world full of suffering, how can one keep living on without concern? I have to leave."

"I knew this day was coming," she said. "So today is the day?"

"Yes. We might meet again or maybe not. But please don't think I don't love you."

"I know."

Thus Siddhartha left for a lonely and difficult journey.

Yaśodharā didn't cry, the author wrote, because she knew that this was his calling. She and their son went on to live a meaningful, fulfilled life, eventually becoming a nun and monk following the Buddhist way. This author's interpretation of this story was very satisfying to me. The author was suggesting that as Buddha left, Yaśodharā herself embarked on a long journey, symbolically, to becoming an independent and wise woman.

Buddha said that you could divide a life into four different periods. The first part is the learning period. The next is the period for working and taking care of your family. The third is the time to leave the family and go into nature to meditate. The fourth period is the time to prepare for death. In this book the author suggests that when you enter the third period, you should live for yourself. Obviously most of us can not leave our family behind. He is talking about spiritual freedom and spiritual independence. That is to say, one should find a way of living that gives you a sense of fulfillment. I know that now is the time for me to enter the third period of my life and discover what form it will take.

The tale about Buddha's wife gave me a new inspiration and courage to start a journey of self-discovery.

About the Author

Fumiko Tokunaga Jensen is a pianist from Japan. She is married to a Danish cellist. As a child she wanted to be a poet or a writer. She accomplishes her childhood dreams as she writes in her third language.

Catherine W. Davis

Introductory Words

I'm an impatient person and I like ideas expressed in as few words as possible. Perhaps this is why I find poetry so appealing. In eighth grade, my best friend gave me a journal, where in between entries I would copy down poems: works by Keats, Shelley, e.e. cummings, Dickinson, Frost, and Shakespeare all found their way onto my pages. Ernest Hemingway was not technically a poet, but I do love his economy of words. I have dabbled in personal essay, creative writing, and flash fiction, but the beauty of writing, for me, lies in the old saying *creativity loves constraint*.

My favorite subjects to write about are my family and northern Michigan, but not necessarily in that order.

Catherine W. Davis

When in Need

In the store I saw something called a "Comfort Bowl."
I had to look. It was meatloaf and mashed potatoes,
    of course.

My own comfort bowl is the blue and white one, shallow,
a carp painted on the inside. I got it for Christmas one year.

When in need, I make fettuccine Alfredo with spinach
and eat it out of my special bowl
while watching an old movie like *Now, Voyager* or *The
    Philadelphia Story.*

At night, after dinner, my husband eats pretzels
    from a little bowl.
Maybe it's his comfort bowl.

One daughter likes deep-dish pizza,
    as circular and deep as a bowl,
when she's feeling down.
The other prefers mashed potatoes on occasion, but only the
    kind she makes herself.

Cheez-Its are my daughter Julia's favorite comfort food,
although once she ate cheese tortellini for dinner every night
    for a month

while she was living in Prague.
Maybe it was comfort food for her. Maybe it was because
she didn't know how to cook anything else.

It was Julia's college graduation yesterday. The last pictures
have been taken, the last goodbyes said
and now I sit buckled into the car, staring out at the
landscape as it rushes by,
a small bag of Cheez-Its in my lap.

I eat them slowly, one by one,
little orange squares of comfort
as the miles spool swiftly away
leaving the past much too far behind, speeding much too
fast toward the future.

The Cottage

In the north woods
Where the tall trees press in on either side
And the owls call at night *who cooks for youuuuuu*

The young lumberjack whistles as he works,
Cutting the trees, fashioning the wood
Into some kitchen shelves for the new cottage going up.

When they first drove up in the Model T
They painted those kitchen shelves white
Brass cup hooks precisely attached
So each heavy white coffee cup with its green stripe
Could have its place.

They sat on the porch steps, looking into the woods
Sipping from the heavy white coffee cup with its green stripe
Staying all summer and into the fall
Leaving only after Christmas was over and it got too cold.

When they pulled up in the Chevrolet
The pot bellied stove that had managed to heat the place into
    December
Was dismantled and placed
In the corner, a relic.

There was a new electric stove now, and
The plumbing was moved indoors
Next to the clawfoot tub which had bathed many children
   and had stood there
Forever. "Some things have to be done," they said.
More cabinets built,
Running water indoors, what progress!

There was a new glider on the porch now, so they could sit
   and look into the woods.

The white shelves still stood where they had been placed,
   not long ago
Brass cup hooks so precisely attached
So each heavy white coffee cup with its green stripe
Could have its place.

And the minivan pulled up
With new children
To dig in the sand of the driveway
And play with the all the strange toys in the toy drawer
Wondering why there was no TV
Briefly, before they ran off to the woods or the beach
Or sit in the glider – who knows how old that thing is?
– to eat their Cheerios out of the cups they found on the
   white shelves

The white shelves which still stood where they had been
   placed, so long ago
Brass cup hooks so precisely attached
So each heavy white coffee cup with its green stripe
Could have its place.

Then the Honda pulled up
And the children watched TV on their phones
But still walked to the beach every afternoon

Or sat in the glider
Looking into the woods.

Although there were less trees now. The neighbors
Cut down most of the ones behind the house
(To build their "retirement paradise." They got divorced a
    year later.)
The light's not the same since they cut down the old
    hemlock.
Another tree fell behind the house this winter.
More will have to come down. Some things have to be done.

The washer and dryer were put in last year, eliminating the
    trip
To town to do the laundry at the laundromat –
Always an adventure involving bags of carefully hoarded
    quarters.

But the white shelves still stand where they had been placed,
    so long ago
Brass cup hooks so precisely attached
So each heavy white coffee cup with its green stripe
Could have its place.

The BMW pulls up
No children get out.
Two people sit on the glider, examining their phones. They
    don't look at the woods.
The peel-and-stick tiles on the kitchen floor, placed there in
    the eighties, have given up the ghost and will have to be
    replaced.
"Let's redo the whole thing," says the husband. "Some
    things have to be done."
The wife cries.
The white shelves, with their carefully placed cup hooks, are
    being taken down.

And Then We Wrote

A young carpenter fashions the wood
Into some shelves for the new kitchen going in
Soon to be painted white
So each heavy white coffee cup with its green stripe
Will have its place.

He whistles as he works.

Catherine W. Davis

Normal: A Sestina

I sit in the kitchen and fold his laundry
Listening to his conference call
Wishing I had someplace to go
Wishing things were normal again
Because I would love to be normal
Because I would love to do some things

I take his folded things
A symbol of my love, his folded laundry
Upstairs. At least this piece of my life is normal
At least it's as normal as I would call.
Next week I'll be right here, again
Waiting for the laundry to go

I certainly have no place to go
No plan to do things
I just go around again
It's time for the laundry
It's time for his next conference call
Passing time, waiting for normal

To occur again. We have lost normal
It has gone to a place we can't go
I call for it, I call
But no reply. Things

Are just about folding laundry
Wanting to be folded again

Tomorrow, and tomorrow again
Creeps in this petty pace, not normal
Except his washing of the laundry
The ordinary world is calling and I must go
At least we can enjoy those things
To be done, which I call

Worthy, as nothing else can I call
Normal. I see myself, again
Holding my head in my hands because things
Are getting out of hand. The return to "normal"
Has become something else. It's time to go
Down to the basement, to heed the call

Of the drying of things; the call
Of my husband's laundry, done again,
The most normal, I guess. I must go.

The Silence

My younger sister sent me a photo the other day
Of a watercolor that hangs on the wall at my mother's house,
A picture of the cottage with grey shingles and red trim
On Cape Cod where we used to go to for a week in late
    August,
The place where my mother spent every August of her
    childhood.
Doesn't this bring up strong memories for you? my sister texts.
    And my answer is ...
No. It doesn't. Why, I'm not sure, except
In the watercolor, there are two planks leaning up against the
    front wall of the cottage. I remember them there. I never
    understood
What their purpose was, and couldn't ask.

My mother's family is of New England stock and if you are of
    good New England stock
You do not discuss things.
There is a deep silence there that keeps you
From asking questions.
My mother's mother died when she was fifteen years old,
The word *cancer* left unsaid, unexplained.
Imagine not knowing how your own mother died
Or not being able to bring it up.
The deep silence seizes you by the throat and chokes you.

And Then We Wrote

My older sister is like this as well
 – I'd like to ask her about certain personal things
But she maintains a silence that stops me every time.
I try but she won't talk about it, or her explanations are vague
And if my mother is in the room, well then –
Forget it. She constantly interrupts with unhelpful sayings like
He'll just grow out of it or *You did the best you could.*
Somehow she thinks it is her fault, how her grandson is.
Then again, she has never been very good at discussing
    anything. There is a deep silence there.
It seizes you by the throat and chokes you.

She doesn't want to talk about leaving her house
Or the things in it. There are too many and she can't part with
    any of them.
The time has come, my sisters and I tell each other.
She's too frail and that house is a millstone around her neck.
Not that she is forgetful or lazy: takes her meds on time and
    goes to the bank as best she can
But she will be ninety next year
And her living situation is getting a little…shifty.
Still, the deep silence
Seizes you by the throat and chokes you.

Today, a storm passed through
Her town. My younger sister is stuck babysitting my mom
After she lost power at the house.
My sister's not texting anymore. We should be
Discussing my mother's next move –
An assisted living place, or hiring someone to come in,
Costs, hours – all the things she would rather not hear.
How we are going to get her to face these details is beyond me.
    There is a deep silence there. It seizes you by
the throat
and chokes
you.

About the Author

Catherine W. Davis was raised a staunch New Englander but has lived in the Chicago area for the last twenty-eight years, making her more of a staunch Midwesterner these days. Two of her favorite poets are Robert Frost and Emily Dickinson, staunch New Englanders themselves. Although she has been known to write in bed and at the kitchen table, her favorite place would be on the porch of her summer cottage in northern Michigan.

Susan E. Cohen

Introductory Words

In sixth grade, without warning, I was summoned to the principal's office. As I started down the hall, I desperately tried to figure out which crime I had unwittingly committed and what horrific punishment awaited me.

It turned out that my teacher had secretly sent my classroom essay to the principal's office. I walked into that room expecting disaster. The principal handed me my essay saying, "My dear, you are a talented writer and you should consider becoming an author when you grow up."

Actually, I must admit that I only write when there is a gun to my head. That gun could be a deadline from an outside source or an emotional experience strong enough to overcome my innate reluctance to put pen to paper.

While in the past, I would do almost anything to avoid starting to write, I have discovered that once I am actually doing it, I feel transported away. It's a special state that is both exciting in the sense that I don't know what is about to pour out, and even pleasurable, because when you're really writing, you feel like you're "in the zone."

Susan E. Cohen

How Can I Marry You?

How can I marry you?
You are not me.
You a man's man…
With your cigars, your ball games,
Your political "hebejebe" talk.

And I an avowed feminist
Who still loves shopping,
Immersed in modern dance
And addicted to a white-scalloped teapot.

You and I are from separate planets.
What madness propels us to descend
(Fragilely armored as we are)
From our lofty separate spheres

And briefly unite just long enough
To recite vows, buy dishes, beget children,
And grow old enough to rattle our rocking chairs
Or whatever it is the grownups do.

And Then We Wrote

What type of strange, interplanetary language
Can we possibly devise
Sufficient enough to merge
Your land riveted scarecrow body
With my floating sea tendril self?

In the dark
Unobserved by our respective allies
We must meet on a wild plain,
Crawl to a small patch of deserted neutral soil,
Our hands clinging to souvenir shards of our own planets;
Our souls clanging together like terrestrial magnets.

Susan E. Cohen

The Secret Life Cycle of My Underpants

I'm sure most people, provided they're not confined to prison or engaged in waging war, have special morning rituals—the hot beverage we look forward to starting the day with or the newspaper we like to scan at the breakfast table. For me it's the special moment when I select the underpants I'm going to wear that day from the very top drawer of a rather tall but narrow brown wicker chest.

In order to select the proper underpants for the day, I do a quick casual psychological scan of my physical well-being as well as my mental status. Every day is unique and so my underpants have to match my state of mind. I actually have a large collection of underwear because our daughter used to belong to the Victoria's Secret Club. For a while there, she received a coupon every month for a free pair of panties. She was not interested in this opportunity, so after a few months of having to discard the unredeemed coupons, I decided that I would take advantage of them. This went on for a couple of years, until I ended up amassing quite a collection.

One important factor in the selection process is attuning the underpants to the season. There are some prints I only wear in winter—the dark navy print with pale blue moons and miniature forest creatures, the pale orange ones with the white deer and tiny snowflakes, the pink ones with large silver snowflakes design, for example. Then there are the summer undies, the lush pastel ones with a tropical print, the hot pink ones with the fish swimming on them, and the pair with vines and flowers growing vertically that remind me of Japanese art.

Some days I need comforting so that's when I put on the pale gray ones with the pink hearts or the white ones with purple, pink and aqua tiny hearts. I also have a pair of paisley undies that remind me of my Mom since she adored paisley prints. Once in a while, if I'm facing a scary day, I might wear them for some hidden emotional support.

Most of the time my underpants live a life of attentive leisure, like firemen hanging around just playing cards at the station, yet remaining alert in case they are called into duty! Nevertheless, my underpants, which are basically on vacation for several days at a time, lead a life of deceptive ease.

Like prostitutes of olden times lounging around a red and gold wallpapered lobby, they recline until they are chosen. And on a particular day, if they are selected and thereby recruited for active duty, they realize they will be quite busy, first shaping themselves to fit my form, and then having to accompany me on whatever missions I endeavor to undertake.

They may be stretched to the limit in a yoga pose or sat on for a few dull hours at my desk, or possibly paraded outside (under other garments, of course) and called to serve on an impossibly chilly or unbearably hot day. Beyond the extremes of temperature they are forced to endure, they are constantly pulled down and up innumerable times day and night as, alas, with maturity I travel to the bathroom more frequently.

And what pair of flowered or lace-trimmed panties does not secretly yearn to be ripped off by an inflamed suitor (or husband as the case may be) and hurled in an amusement park ride manner across the bed to observe limply from the floor the private relations of the intimate parts it has so valiantly been working to conceal.

In addition to having to cover all of the nether regions of the body, these beleaguered clothing items must also prepare themselves to be scooped up and unceremoniously dumped without warning into a washing machine, which must certainly provoke nightmarish thoughts of being drowned, while being swished this way and that, and in a final spurt of indignity, spun around at a daringly high speed until they are twisted into wet rags gasping for breath and barely alive. Then, of course, they do get rescued, and I gently unfold each one and drape its wet, exhausted form over the dryer rack which serves to clearly mark me as old fashioned for not simply tossing them in the dryer.

Most days, by the end of the day I've totally forgotten which pair I'm wearing, as believe it or not, I do have other things on my mind! But late at night, when I finally do undress and thereby reveal the panties, there is a moment of recognition and remembrance of the start of that day, about where I was in my consciousness that led me to choose a particular pair that morning. And, in the end, each pair gets pressed and folded and returns to looking quite pristine again, so it can be lovingly laid to rest and given time to recover in its honored top drawer wicker sanctuary.

Modesty

Because my mother was a tomboy, I ended up having to sleep in sensible tailored blue pajamas instead of the frilly nightgowns that I coveted. It had simply never occurred to my mother that her daughter might not be made exactly in her image. She could not conceive of the possibility that her daughter might like dolls as a child, even though she personally had no use for them. It was beyond her imagination that I might covet shiny black patent leather shoes; my mother was a fervent proponent of sturdy sensible brown lace-up oxfords.

So when our family was invited to a relative's wedding out of town, I wondered what kind of garments that would normally violate my mother's religion of function I might finally have a chance to wear. To my eight-year old delight I was allowed to pick out a pink dress and, in the style of the day, I was also the proud owner of a "stick out slip."

This was really a type of petticoat with many layers of gauze attached to rows of ribbons. There were multiple layers of stiff material topped by an elastic waistband so the net result was that it made the lower half of your dress stand out around you for a veritable Scarlett O'Hara effect. I am sure that both the dress and the crinolines were a bit generously sized so that I could grow into them, as just about every item of clothing I owned was purchased with the idea that it had better fit for more than the current season.

My brother and I listened to any tidbit of news about the

upcoming wedding, because in our quiet small world, social events of this type were rare. I knew that there would be a real band and lots of tasty food, and I imagined swirling around in my pink dress like the ballerina I longed to be. Even though I spent my childhood twirling around the house to music and improvising all sorts of dance movements, I was one of the only girls among my friends that did not get to take ballet lessons as my mother deemed them unnecessary.

Similarly, even though a piano purchased by my grand-mother was one of our few possessions, we were never offered lessons. My mother had been forced by her mother to take lessons so she decided, without ever consulting either my brother or me, to simply spare us the unnecessary expense of something she had not enjoyed. But none of that mattered now--I was going to a real wedding and wearing a pink dress and even dress shoes, so my excitement knew no limits.

It was a splendid affair, but something went wrong. Upon arrival I discovered that all of the "grown-ups" were seated at round tables of about ten. There were several long tables that had been set up for the younger guests. I searched the place cards for my name or my brother's at the "kids table," but could not find our seats. When I circled back to our parents, I discovered that my mother did not want our relatives to have to pay for two individual "extra" meals for her children.

That would have been a waste of good money, so she had frugally instructed them to skip our meals; we could just sit with our parents and nibble off their plates. I remember watching all the other kids having fun at the designated chil-dren's tables, as the realization that somehow we did not ap-pear to matter as much as everyone else slowly pervaded my consciousness.

I decided not to dwell on our "foreign status" and have as good a time as possible out on the dance floor. I had made it to the wedding in a pink dress and even though I had never had lessons, I knew that I could really dance. Most of the numbers were meant for couples, but at one point everyone formed a conga line for the "bunny hop." We all put our hands on the shoulders of the person in front of us and hopped in unison to the fervent beat of the band. I was caught up in the pure primal rhythm of it all as my black braids bounced on my back. I was finally in a situation where I looked like I belonged. After all, no one could tell that we were banished to our parents' table out on the dance floor in the midst of the pulsing music and pounding beat.

And then it happened, one minute I was jumping in my patent leather shoes and pink dress, and then in a split second I had jumped out of my white stick out slip which now stood on the dance floor like a fluffy white tent. I turned red--no one was supposed to know that I was wearing such an undergarment, but there it stood behind me--exhibit A--living proof that I had been wearing a slip and, if so, probably underpants as well and God only knew what was under those!

It seems impossible in this day and age, when young women proudly flaunt their bra straps and pregnant women display their "bumps," but there was a time when all of ladies underwear was referred to as "unmentionables" for a reason. If ¼ inch of slip happened to hang below the hemline of your dress, this was considered a flaw that must be instantly corrected. And yet there was one of my unmentionables blatantly exposed on the shiny wood of the dance floor. Since I was right in front of it, it was quite evident whom that half slip belonged to, not to mention the fact that the skirt of my cherished formerly ballerina-like pink dress now hung limply down my slim undeveloped hips.

I did not have the perspective of maturity to know that the whole world or the guests of this wedding were not particularly shocked by the fact that I had literally jumped out of my petticoat. As far as I was concerned, I was humiliated, I was exposed, I was the Scarlet Woman who now might be summoned for a witch burning.

If I could have looked into the future, I would have understood that this was the most minor infringement of "wardrobe malfunction," as we term it today, imaginable. If I had known what postures I would be forced to assume at some far out future year at the gynecologist or the ultimate exposure of childbirth in the delivery room, I would have laughed out loud.

But at eight years old, I retreated to the women's bathroom with hot tears on my cheeks. There in the privacy of a stall, with one quick pull up I was able to reassemble my apparel, but I knew in the deepest recesses of my formerly pure soul, that there had been a public breach of manners and an irretrievable violation of my modesty.

The Importance of Radar

As carefully as a dog watches any human being in sight, I watched my father. In other words, I studied him until I developed some extra keen sense so highly evolved, so sensitive, so focused that it approached the status of a technologically advanced radar device.

Dogs have made an art of observing us, because any slight error on our part, constitutes a potential treat. Much more rare, but most delightful of all, the possibility of a clumsy human accidentally dropping a piece of chicken or absentmindedly leaving an entire roast on an unguarded table may present the opportunity of a lifetime! But for me, watching my father became a necessary tool I felt I needed to arm myself with in order to ensure my survival.

You see, my mother did not watch my father. She grew up in a calm loving atmosphere and therefore was not on the lookout for warning signs. From a young age, I scanned my father's face continually, searching for signs of tension, for a slight reddening of the skin, a tautness in the facial muscles, for any minuscule difference in the expression of his eyes. My mother, even after having said something that obviously irritated him, blithely continued down the same dangerous conversational path. She was unfortunately not equipped with the yellow and red caution lights that had already started intermittently flashing in my brain.

My brother was equally oblivious and seemed to somehow

delight in provoking my father's wrath. He would start some sort of trivial trouble at the dinner table, and instantly my warning system would go on high alert. As I watched my father's anger start to grow, I would silently pray that some higher power would intercede. My brother, however, seemed encouraged by the tiny sprouts of anger he had just planted and would start feeding, cultivating and watering them until they grew into some sort of an evil plant monstrosity. No winged god ever intervened.

My brother seemed to know he was safe. When my father would reach the boiling point with my brother, he would then turn this rage onto my mother. My brother seemed perversely satisfied: now the sparks would fly and he could enjoy his role of creator. He had, in fact, acquired a certain amount of power by making something happen. Within a previously quiet, neutral space, he had been able to convert sparks into fire.

I managed to stay out of the line of fire by being so outrageously "good" that, in retrospect, it horrifies me to remember. My father never yelled at me. I never got spanked or scolded or even frowned on. I was too aware of the force that my father's anger could unleash. So somehow, even as a young child, I made the decision to be good no matter the cost.

When my brother and I squabbled over who would get to sit in the front seat of the car with our father, my father would prevail on my maturity. I was, after all, a full year and one half older, and a girl besides, and therefore expected to yield to my brother. My father would offer the explanation that my brother would be more upset than I would if he didn't get his way. It seems that my father learned early on that he could somehow appeal to my budding "Buddha nature" and therefore count on me to relinquish my position.

There was not anything my father would not do for his children, except perhaps control his temper, which to be fair was something of which he had no awareness. Neither he nor my mother realized the possible pain their fighting might inflict on their offspring. Once when I was twelve or thirteen, after a particularly bad explosion, my father found me quietly sobbing in my room. What I remember most was how shocked he was that I could possibly have been even slightly affected by his behavior.

My mother did not realize the impact of their fighting until she was about 97 and happened to read a newspaper advice column on the subject. She asked me if growing up, I had noticed any of their altercations and was possibly bothered by them. You see, we grew up in a time when children were thought to be relatively oblivious; it was not exactly a time of psychological awareness. Somehow many parents thought their children were protected by an invisible glass bubble and, therefore, shielded from whatever radioactive fallout their marital relationship produced.

When you have a father who rages, who is capable of yelling or violently erupting or even occasionally shattering dishes, you may vow to never marry a man who would possibly behave like that. In the presence of men, whether it's a salesperson, a boss, a clergyman or a guy you picked up in a bar, you listen more carefully, you watch more closely, you are on guard for telltale signs. How does this man act in the presence of others, how does he respond in an exchange with a stranger, how does he deal with frustration?

When you have a father who rages, you are, in fact, always on alert. You acquire a tendency to scan the room for any signs of trouble so that you can intercede in those rare instances when there is a possibility of heading off a disturbance and making a temporary but fragile peace. You become what we would call hypervigilant, scanning the family atmosphere for any subtle warning signs, a youngster running your own personal airport traffic control system.

Eventually, you develop a surveillance system so keen that it rivals the way your dog watches you. Consider how a dog knows when you're about to take a walk or head towards the treat bag or can sense someone arriving at your house long before your human senses detect anything happening at all.

Out of self-defense you also become a veritable scanner of human beings, as you come to understand and appreciate the supreme importance of radar.

A Sumptuous Death

The only good death I can possibly attempt to visualize would be a little out of the ordinary. Let's face it, while the death of everyone we know is a scary thought, and the death of anyone close to us is a horrific, terrifying nightmare-inducing thought, the death of oneself is a virtually unthinkable thought.

I have always cherished privacy, so one would think I would prefer to depart life from home, safely tucked between the comfy covers of our bed. However, as I gave it a moment's serious consideration, what came to mind is that I would much prefer to die at the ocean.

And if it's going to be at the seashore, only a summer death would be fitting, because I definitely don't want to die cold. I mean I'll be cold enough once I'm dead, but I won't be conscious then and I'm sure that my spirit will migrate somewhere warm and no, I am not thinking Hell. However, if I make a tropical destination my deathbed, that would work year round. Since very few of us get to choose the season of our death, I should best prepare by immediately moving to and enjoying such a locale while awaiting the inevitable.

So I'm at the beach and wearing something light and loose and comfortable--no holding in one's tummy when death is approaching--I mean who wants to die in an underwire bra and pantyhose or high heels and earrings? Which means that I probably should completely cease wearing any of the above items at once, just to be prepared.

Being at the beach there would probably be no doctors or nurses around, unless they happen to be on vacation, in which case they probably are not going to try and resuscitate me, as that would only turn into a possible legal nightmare. And it would wipe out having any IV's or monitors--I had enough of those in childbirth.

So there would be no machines, feverishly charting one's declining heart rate, brain function or oxygen levels, for those present to focus on, rather than actually attending to the dying person. This would, of course, necessitate accepting death as a more natural process, which is exactly what most of us are trying our hardest to avoid.

Also, I'd have a good supply of morphine in my beach tote, because, after all, who needs a painful death? If I had known better, I would have brought my own drugs to the delivery room. I may as well make use of that hard won wisdom, and as I am not likely to produce any more offspring, at least apply it to the dying process.

Even if I were too weak to sit up, I would still be able to smell the salt air, hear the sea gulls, and watch the waves. Why if I had the luxury of a protracted death, I would rent a house by the sea and invite my friends from various stages of life to come visit and say everything we don't ordinarily speak, when we think we are going to continue living on forever.

I would ask each person to please just bring flowers and hopefully, to make that visit happen before I died, not after. I'd press those blossoms to my face, remembering how the delicacy of each one was a unique pleasure. And it would be so delightful, reminiscing and bidding each other heartening farewells, that each visit would possibly prolong my life for at least a few more days.

The more I think of it, you might as well leave life wanting more of it, which is far more likely to happen by the ocean during the summer. In winter if you are really freezing and your car won't start, you may not care that much if you get taken out. But it's very hard to not want to keep living--the only time I can really remember feeling like that was in the throes of labor, when I fantasized about a red button on the wall that you could press and just end those moments of agony.

But most of the time, even when we are depressed or discouraged or just going through rough times, we don't really want to end it all because the compassionate force instilled in us a resilient cockeyed optimism that urges us to believe that things will get better, if we can just hang in there.

But anyway, back to the beach--it would be nice to be distracted by waves, each one different and entirely unpredictable. That is how I lived through each attempted natural childbirth--pretending each contraction was just a wave that one only went through once, one at a time. Luckily there are only a finite number of waves in childbirth and that would be the only way I could conceive of death. That each of us gets to witness a finite number of waves, even though the ocean goes on forever.

It would also be good to not have to die hungry, why even vicious criminals on death row are given a last supper of their choosing. Since it's hard to predict the exact day of anyone's death, I would be certain to make every meal an indulgent banquet, returning back to that magnificent era not long past when all of us were not counting calories or cholesterol or meal points or referring to the glycemic index.

I would plunge into eating the pleasure foods, ignoring the virtuous souls around me who are all immersed in being vegan or keto or macrobiotic or paleo, and those watching "The Biggest Loser," in order to prepare for eternal life.

I would remember that time as a teenager that I went swimming in the ocean for hours, not feeling cold, not feeling any urge to come back to the land, just immersing myself in the water. And then I separate from the sea and emerge dripping wet, feeling suddenly freezing and wet and hungry and wrapping myself in a giant soft towel. I recall there was a nearby stand with hot salty french fries, real ones, and re-membering how I let each hot greasy succulent wedge of po-tato melt in my mouth, thinking it does not get better than this...

About the Author

Susan E. Cohen is an aspiring combination writer, poet, artist and perpetual student, who loves to study medicine and is fascinated by art, psychology and religion. In her early twenties, she became severely and then chronically ill with an unknown disease now called ME/CFS while conducting a research project for her doctorate. Her family consists of a fly-fishing husband, three adult children who collectively named her "The Dalai Mama," and Banjo the dog.

Brian Harrison

Introductory Words

I have flirted with writing throughout my life, but with little success. No one has ever encouraged me to quit my day job to concentrate on my writing. I heeded this non-encouragement and I kept my day job until I retired.

And Now I Write.

Over the years I have puttered in many different genres. Never settling on any one genre for full-time puttering.

The T-bone Trilogies and "The Tree Whisperer" are from the memoir I tell people I am writing. They are pieces I have written in retirement. They share the same style and voice. My voice.

"The White Wolf" was written before I quit my day job. It is a darker genre than I normally dabble.

"The Ox Lost His Sock" is my first and last attempt at a poem. As poetry goes it is as clumsy as an ox. But that's part of its charm.

I hope you enjoy.

The T-bone Trilogies

Part One
The Huckleberry Patch

I was sitting in a huckleberry patch, in the shadows of the line of Lombardy poplars that marked the western edge of our farm. I was grazing like a fatted calf on huckleberries when my brother T-bone found me. Standing at the edge of the patch, my older brother by two years, waved a book of matches above his head and calls out, "Ghana oak jiggers' rats?"

I stared back at my nine-year old brother and I crinkled my face judgmentally, "I don't think Mom and Dad would like that."

T-bone scowled. "Wag other doing think," he snapped in T-bone-ese, a language that only my brother spoke. The closest related language to T-bone-ese was spoken by a small group of Haitian-born carnies in Denmark in the 1920s, a language that died when the last of them passed away in 1972, only to be revived in the later stages of the twentieth century by a boy with a speech impediment. T-bone-ese, when spoken by my brother was understood by no one, except for me and my little sister, Lulu. We were his interpreters whenever T-bone conversed with an adult. Of the two, I was the better translator. My five-year-old sister did not understand the nuances or the verb conjugations of T-bone-ese. She did not grasp the fact that T-bone-ese is a word-poor language and, as such, relies heavily on phrases and facial expressions. Lulu's biggest transgression, however, was her propensity to misinterpret words. Sometimes deliberately and for her own benefit. Fortunately, no one truly believed that T-bone wanted Lulu to have his ice cream. Or that T-bone thought it was very important that his little sister got the last piece of cake.

But as I was saying, I was sitting in the huckleberry patch when T-bone found me. He held up a book of matches and said in T-bone-ese, "Do you want to smoke a cigarette?"

I looked up at my brother and shook my head, "I don't think Mom and Dad would like that."

T-bone scowled. "Dad doesn't let us do anything!" he snapped.

Curious, I got up and joined T-bone at the edge of the huckleberry patch. "You found cigarettes?" I asked.

"No," he said in T-bone-ese.

"If you don't got a cigarette how are we going to smoke?" I asked.

My brother said in T-bone-ese, but I will translate for the sake of brevity, "I don't have a cigarette but that's the good thing. 'Cause, it's the tobacco that is the cancer-causing agent. We don't want to smoke no tobacco. What I got here is wintergreen."

"Wintergreen?" I repeated.

"Yes, it's a mint. I just picked it. But here is the dilemma," my brother explained in his native language. "We have no proper papers to wrap the mint in. A cigarette would be handy. We could cannibalize the cigarette by taking the tobacco out of the paper and replace it with wintergreen."

"What about a pipe?" I suggested.

T-bone rolled his eyes. "Where are we going to get a pipe? Dad doesn't smoke."

"Uncle Tom has some. He has a lot of them in his room," I offered.

T-bone scowled, "And how do you suggest we get them? They're in town at Grandma's house."

"Oh yeah," I said sheepishly and headed back into the huckleberry patch.

"Hey… where do you think you are going?" T-bone howled in T-bone-ese.

"I'm going to eat huckleberries," I said peevishly. "You come and ask me if I wanted to smoke a cigarette, but you don't have a cigarette and that's a good thing because you have wintergreen, except you don't have any papers or a pipe to put it in. Given the two choices I've decided to go back to eating huckleberries."

"No. Wait! I got papers." T-bone cried, holding up the back cover of Dad's *Fortune* magazine.

Interested, I returned. "Does Dad know that you got his magazine?"

"No, but I just got the back page. Not the cover," T-bone said in T-bone-ese. "And besides, this is an old one. Dad's already read it."

T-bone tore off a part of the magazine and dropped to his knees. He took the mint out of his pocket and tried to wrap it in the glossy paper. It was difficult but with enough spit T-bone was able to manufacture a semblance of a cigarette. It was about the size of a Jamaican spliff.

"Ghana rye erst," T-bone asked.

"No, I'm good. You can go first," I said. "I'll light the match for you."

I lit the first match and the wind blew it out. I turned away from the wind and lit the second match. The wind blew that one out too. The third match would not light at all. On the fourth match, with T-bone and me huddled together, hunched over and away from the wind we finally got it lit. T-bone leaned in. I put the fire to the cigarette and the paper burst into flames. The fire leaped at T-bone's face and singed his eyebrows. He dropped the cigarette and the wind swept up the burning fragments of the *Fortune* magazine and scattered them into the huckleberry patch. We frantically raced through the patch stamping out the smoldering ambers. When all the fires were extinguished, we rolled another wintergreen cigarette and tried it again. With the same results, I'm afraid, except this time it was my eyebrows that got burnt. That was enough for me. I walked away from T-bone and went back to eating huckleberries.

The T-bone Trilogies

Part Two
Oh Canada

We were riding in my father's Wagoneer heading to Toronto, Canada. I had just killed off a large root beer soda. My bladder was about to burst when my mother turned and asked if we needed to use the bathroom before we crossed the border. She pointed her chin toward Lulu to signify that my little sister was to answer. Lulu, being a suck-up, knew Dad was agitated by how long it took us to get out of Chicago and what a pain in the ass it was getting through road construction in Kalamazoo. She knew from Dad's grousing that he wanted to get through the Detroit-Windsor tunnel before rush hour or we'd be stuck in long lines.

"I'm good," the little suck-up replied.

My mother's chin then pointed at T-bone who was sitting between me and Lulu. "Do you need to go, T-bone?'

"By tag tinkle what by at tag can a Doug," T-bone replied.

My mother's eyes immediately turned to me as she pointed her chin in my direction. I sighed, "T-bone says he needs to go a little, but he can wait until we get to Canada."

"That settles it," my father exclaimed, as he hit the accelerator and swerved into the fast lane.

"Wait," I cried, "I've got to go."

Either my parents did not hear me or believed that my bladder was outvoted by the other bladders in the car, and I would have to accept the consequences. That's just how democracy works, buster.

I held on the best I could until we crossed the border and pulled into a gas station. I jumped out and ran to the restroom.

"T-bone go follow your brother," I heard my mother order as I raced to the nearest urinal. T-bone slid across the seat and out the door I had burst from.

I was already at the urinal when T-bone moseyed in. He went to the urinal next to mine and chuckled, "Dis hob lick bow ant."

To the rest of the occupants in the washroom, my brother's words must have sounded as foreign and garbled as French-Canadian. They had no idea what he said.

I understood T-bone and wrinkled my face. "Why is this an historic moment?" I asked, still peeing out a steady stream of recycled root beer.

T-bone replied in T-bone-ese, but I will translate for the sake of clarity, "This is our first pee in Canada," he said. "We're going to remember this moment for the rest of our lives."

I have traveled much since that day and have peed in many different countries. With every first pee I think of Canada. Most first pees are in airports and are not all that memorable. One airport restroom looks pretty much like another. There is only one other pee I can remember, my first pee in Russia. It was in a train station just across the border on our way to Leningrad from Helsinki. There was a small window just above the urinal. It looked out into the courtyard and to a giant poster of Vladimir Lenin. His eyes seemed suspiciously fixated on me while I urinated.

A crusty old woman was scowling at me from the row of sinks. She worked for tips, handing out paper towels and cleaning the stalls and urinals. She did not seem happy in her profession; glowering at me as if I was a cheap-ass foreigner who did not appreciate the dignity of her work. I placed a handful of Swedish kronor into her tip jar as I was leaving. Thinking I was an American and hoping for a tip in dollars she was less than thrilled with my kronor. She scowled and mumbled under her breath, "You suck," in perfect T-bone-ese.

The Ox Lost His Sock

The Ox lost his sock.
Not all, mind you, just one.
He put it in a box.
He was sure he had.
He was almost certain of it.
He was even quite sure which box.
He stared at the box with his sock and began to sob.
For the box had a lock and the lock had a key.
The Ox knew just where his key would be.
It was where he always kept it.
Inside his sock.
The one inside the box.
The Ox lost his sock.
Not all, mind you, just one.

The T-bone(-ish) Trilogies

Part Three
The Thanksgiving Play

A few months after T-bone and I nearly burned our faces off trying to smoke cigarettes and a week before Thanksgiving, my older sister Mary came to the younger siblings and asked if we wanted to be in a Thanksgiving play she wrote. To entice us my sister added, "If we're good enough maybe we can perform it at Grandma's house on Thanksgiving."

We loved Grandma and loved her home. She had sweets and straws and flavored tablets that fizzed when plopped into water. We had none of those things at home. Grandma's kitchen had exotic foods like toffee, caramel and Ovaltine. Foods that were strangers to my mother's pantry.

My grandmother was kind and generous. She allowed us to graze in her kitchen. We only had to ask nicely, and we could have practically anything we desired. I learned to ask nicely at a very young age.

My grandmother's house was old and fun to explore. The house had many relics. Old dresses and shoes for dress up, and plenty of do-dads and what-cha-ma-call-its to study and examine but the best thing about Grandma's house was Uncle Tom's refrigerator. Uncle Tom was the youngest of my father's brothers. He stayed with Grandma after Grandpa died. He was our favorite uncle. Mostly because he was nice to us, but the refrigerator tipped the scales in his favor. Uncle Tom's refrigerator was always stocked with soda for the kids and beer for the men. There was not just one kind of soda either, there was always a variety. He had Coke, and ginger ale, root beer, and Squirt, and sometimes Mountain Dew. We never had sodas at home.

"It's not in the budget," my father would bellow.

Uncle Tom's refrigerator was legendary among every child and beer-drinking adult.

Grandma's house was always fun, but Thanksgiving was the best. Grandma was a great cook. Her turkey was always moist and tender. Her mashed potatoes and gravy were no mere side dish. She elevated the common starch into the food for the Gods. All the kids scrambled for seconds.

My father refrained from the potatoes and gravy, pushing them away, declaring, "I don't want to fill up on potatoes when there's Grandma's apple pie."

Grandma made the best apple pie in the county and had the blue ribbons to prove it. Her pie crust was the envy of the county fair. Her secret was lard. An ingredient that won her ribbons but may have contributed to Grandpa's early heart attack.

If Grandma's cooking and Uncle Tom's refrigerator were not enough, Thanksgivings brought together all our cousins. Apart from my oldest sister Pam and the baby there was nearly a cousin for each of my siblings and me. My brother Gizmo, who had just started high school, hung out with Johnny, who was in the same grade as my sisters Mary and Lisa. T-bone paired up with cousin David, they were the same age. I'm not sure David understood a thing T-bone uttered, but he was a good sport about it.

My cousin was Jeff, Johnny's little brother. He was six, a year younger than me and the same age as my sister Lulu, but he was more sophisticated than she was. Jeff understood irony as a tool of comedic storytelling. He loved my stories. Lulu said they were dumb.

Jeff's favorite of my stories was "The Adventures of Sir Snots-a-Lot," the intrepid Kleenex tissue on a knightly quest to rid the world of snot. The stories were unrefined and gross, but they were comedy gold to us. By the end of the story we'd be rolling on the floor laughing and holding our potbellies.

My sisters, Mary, who was fourteen, and Lisa, who was nearly twelve-and-a-half, had to share their cousin. Susan was the only girl their age. We were used to sharing. It's something you learn when you are from a big family.

My cousin Gale wanted to play with Mary, Lisa, and Susan, but she was too young and was stuck with Lulu, which wasn't a good fit. Gale found Lulu annoying. Gale liked to read and Lulu liked to yap.

My father called Lulu Duck-a-loo, or Duck for short. He said this was because Lulu quacked like a duck when she spoke. Lulu never quacked around us, but when Dad was in the room, the little suck-up perfected her quackery.

When Mary asked us if we wanted to be in the play, Lulu jumped at the chance. "I'll do it. I'll do it," she squealed, not quacked.

Lisa agreed to be in the play, but T-bone said no. I was hesitant too. I wanted to see the script. I wanted to know the character I'd be playing.

Mary handed me four pages of loose-leaf paper stapled together with the edges rumpled. "You play the turkey," she stated.

As I read through the script it occurred to me that the turkey was the star. He did not have the most lines, he had only one. But it was the most important line. It was the punchline sure to have the audience howling. And I, as the turkey, would be delivering the line that will bring the house down.

"I'll do it," I declared.

Reluctantly, and with much coercion, T-bone agreed to play the role of the strong but mostly silent farmer. Lisa played the farmer's wife. Mary and Lulu were the farmer's children and I was their pet turkey.

"Pure typecasting," my father roared when he heard of my part.

The play was no Shakespeare, but since Shakespeare never wrote an American Thanksgiving play, I can state with certainty that Mary's play was on par with any Thanksgiving play Shakespeare never wrote.

The play was simple. We staged it in Grandma's living room. The audience of uncles, aunts, cousins, my father, and Gizmo were on the other side of the room spilling over into the adjacent dining room. The younger cousins were sprawled on the floor in front of the stage. Grandma was summoned from the kitchen to take her seat in her favorite rocking chair. My mother and Pam remained in the kitchen preparing dinner. They had seen the play in rehearsal and knew it sucked.

We were a low budget theater group. My turkey costume consisted of construction paper made to look like feathers which was pinned to the back of my trousers. Our only prop was an axe T-bone made from scraps of wood and aluminum foil.

The play began with the farmer, his two daughters and the turkey sitting together having a good laugh when the farmer's wife enters with a solemn look. "I'm sorry but we have no turkey for tomorrow's Thanksgiving dinner."

"Oh no," the girls shouted. "What are we going to do? Thanksgiving is not the same without turkey on our plate."

The farmer's wife shrugged her shoulders and looked aggrieved but said, "I see no alternative. Farmer T-bone, please take the turkey to Grandma's kitchen and have him slaughtered and gutted."

"Oh no," the girls screamed.

This was where I was instructed to pretend I'm biting my nails. Because apparently turkeys bite their nails when they are nervous.

My acting paid off. The audience laughed without me

saying a word. I was feeling pretty good about myself. I knew I was going to deliver the final line so flawlessly the crowd would go wild.

"Oh, no," the girls cried as the play continued, "not our turkey. He's our friend."

The farmer's wife spoke softly and sympathetically to the girls, "I know he's your friend. I like him too. But it's Thanksgiving. We always have turkey on Thanksgiving. It's our tradition."

The two girls looked down gloomily and said, "You're right, Momma. Thanksgiving wouldn't be the same without a turkey."

This was T-bone's cue to pick up his axe, place it over his shoulder, walk over to me and say, "Um."

I dropped my head, slumped my shoulders and followed farmer T-bone dejectedly to the kitchen. Before we got out of the living room the farmer's wife yelled, "No, stop. Don't kill the turkey! I found hot dogs in Uncle Tom's freezer."

This shattered the tension. The crowd thinking it was the end of the play, gave a raucous applause. T-bone and I scrambled back to the stage as Mary announced, "This is the next day at our Thanksgiving dinner."

The farmer's wife held up a glass to make a toast, "What a wonderful Thanksgiving dinner. Good food and good friends and family. What do you say, turkey?"

This was my line and I was ready. I was about to say it when Lulu quacked, "It's better than eating me!"

Her tone and timing were impeccable. She nailed it and the house exploded with laughter. Uncle Tom laughed so hard he spewed beer through his nose. Aunt Ruth dropped her cigarette into her martini, and Grandma nearly fell out of her chair.

"How cute," Aunt Kathy snorted, "the little duckling stole the show from the turkey."

This set off a new round of laughter.

Meanwhile, the action on stage continued when the turkey

jumped up, stomped over to the youngest of the farmer's daughters and punched her right in the shoulder.

"That was my line! You dirty duck," the turkey squawked.

The turkey reared back and was about to strike again, when the farmer's daughter dashed off stage and ran to the kitchen yelling, "Mommy, the turkey is hitting me! The turkey is hitting me!"

The turkey chased the farmer's daughter off the stage and through the audience, clucking more like a chicken than a turkey, "You stole my line! You dirty duck! You stole my line!"

The White Wolf

My condition was terminal. Every doctor told me so. My dreams did too. I was haunted every night by a large white wolf that stalked me in my sleep; waiting, as all predators do, for his prey to grow feeble.

I heard his howls and sensed his stare. On my weakest nights I felt his breath and could hear the cackling of a hyena in the distance, waiting for her turn to scavenge my bones. It was only a matter of time before the fangs of the white wolf would be at my neck.

One day my wife got the news her mother was dying, I could not fully take care of myself, so my twin brother came to stay with me.

On the second night of my brother's stay I dreamed we were walking in the woods, on a path along a stream. Suddenly, I spotted the wolf and pushed my brother behind a tree. The wolf charged. I crouched down and prepared to die but the beast raced past. He brought down a hyena instead. The hyena shrieked and whimpered until it was dead.

I was praying the wolf had not seen us when my cell phone went off. The beast rose from his bloody feast and peered toward the sound. He sprang for the kill, but before he could strike, my phone rang again and awoke me from my slumber.

It was my wife. Her mother had died. I could not help but think that her mother was the hyena in my dream, but I dared not say it.

I barely slept the rest of the night. In the morning I found my brother dead. Doctors say it was a heart attack. I know it was the wolf. I left the dream before my time and the wolf took my twin instead.

My condition is no longer terminal. The white wolf no longer haunts my dreams.

The Tree Whisperer

As a recent retiree I was worried I'd find myself untethered to the workweek. Friends who are retired often forget what day it is. They tell me that they really don't care, it's all the same to them. Though I am not tied to the Monday to Friday workweek, I am tethered to Thursday. For Thursday is Savanah Banana day. It's the day when my four-year-old granddaughter Savanah stays with us.

With her older siblings in school, it was determined that Savanah would not be put in daycare. Instead she is schlepped among parents and grandparents. Thursday is our day. My wife works at home on Thursday, assuring that Savanah has some semblance of adult supervision. My job is to entertain Savanah while my wife is on conference calls. On nice days I take Savanah to the park or a nature center. On bad days we go to the library or stay home and watch *Peppa Pig*. Right now, while the weather is pleasant we are exploring playgrounds around the area.

Savanah is smart, but without the cynicism of her eleven-year-old brother. She believes much of what I tell her. She doesn't understand, just yet, that her grandfather often wanders in the land of the ludicrous.

One day while we were walking in the park, the wind blew and the leaves on the trees fluttered. I told her about Marlo, a character in one of my stories who could talk to trees. I told her that trees talk in two ways: the first by their systems of roots, speaking through pulsations in the ground; the second through the rustling of leaves on windy days. I said that Marlo had feet, not roots, so he was not privy to the conversations underground. But he did understand the trees when their banter went airborne. Trees love to gossip in the wind.

I took my granddaughter to walk the Savanna Trail at our local nature center. It is a trail, I say, that is named after her. We were walking the path when Savanah turned to me and said, "The trees are mad at people."

"Who told you that?" I asked.

"The trees," she said. "They are talking in the wind."

Given the current state of our planet I can believe the trees are mad. I also can believe Savanah understood the trees when they spoke. After all, her grandfather told her it was possible, so she listened when the wind blew. I'm proud Savanah is a tree whisperer, but I am reminded that I must be careful with the stories I spin.

About the Author

On **Brian Harrison**'s tombstone it will be written, "Well! It was fun while it lasted." Brian was born in a small town thirty-five miles north of Michigan's fifth metacarpal. He was the sixth child of eight born in the middle of the baby boom — which is all you need to know about the baby boom. After surviving his teenage years and muddling through most of his twenties, Brian came up with a plan for success and happiness; find a good job and don't screw it up; find a good person to marry and don't screw it up.

Brian's plan was not fully operational until his mid-thirties, but it has been running fairly smoothly ever since. Brian found a job as a computer programmer with the Railroad Retirement Board — a federal bureau he calls *the little agency that could*. Over his twenty-eight-year career Brian rose to the highly esteemed position of mid-level muckety-muck. Brian has been with his wife, Nancy, for over thirty years. He claims that she is the main reason he is having fun while it lasts.

Tony Piggott

Introductory Words

at age forty-three i decided to retire from the world
    of business
to write draw and learn how to paint
seventeen years later i consider myself the luckiest man alive
i write draw or paint everyday
i write to clear my head
most of it is cathartic drivel
in amongst it are the chapters of a very long unfinished book
about love loss joy fear contentment pain bliss tragedy peace
    shame redemption ...
the pieces published here are moments of inspiration
    as they hit
chosen by happenstance
although they seem to have a thread

fire

i want you when you're burning bright
i want your cigarette to light
i want the fire that licks and stings and burns my skin and
    singes wings
i want your fire burning bright
the embers red hot orange white
i want your fire
i want your flame
i want your energy again

i want the smoke to fill my lungs
and burn my throat
and bite my tongue
i want to taste the bitter sweet
tobacco tar
and sizzling meat
your burning bush
your weeds
your trees
alight like forest fires at night
a glow that spreads
a blazing bed of coals
to feed and cleanse my soul
hot fevered body
sweat and blood

a magma molten flood

i want to burn in my desire
i love you when you are on fire
i want you
....

i want you
when you are burnt out
crashed and spurned
and turned out
sad
i want you
when it's all gone bad
the charred remains of bone and ash
in black and white
cold dead and tired
i want you when there is no fire

i want to heat your frozen flesh
i want to be your warm caress
i want to light your cigarette

everything changes nothing

strange as it may seem
change is like a beam of light
there is nothing faster
than a beam of light
right

everything changes
right before my eyes
i see change happening
like now

everything just rearranges
everything rearranged itself
everything is changing

even change
changes
everything
changing
strange how everything changes

everything changes nothing
is a conversation between
    two characters
rat and ant
rat is a rat
ant is a kiwi
they are sitting around
a campfire
by a lake
at the back of beyond
discussing their adventure
so far

my face has changed
a change of face
replacing all
that was
with
this that is
right now

i remember
there wasn't a line
crease
crinkle
or wrinkle
i remember
when skin was tight
smooth
flat
without a groove
but everything changes

funny how things change
like they've changed
between you and me
we used to be
let's say
different

yeah you've changed
strange how you changed
it's almost like you've been rearranged
stacked up differently

when i met you
i thought you were
like little neat boxes
all stacked up
in a kind of ordered fashion
but now
i can see that you are random
a collection of moving parts
all moving as one
changing being
all being as one
being
change

yeah everything is moving
changing my being
being rearranged
changing lanes

i have changed
you've changed
we've all changed

yeah I'm going to go and get changed

i have changed my tune

yeah

change
small change
small changes at first

massive change
change everything

change every thing
change your mind
change what you think
change the way you look
from behind

change who you are
change what you do from now on
change sides
changing tides
change rides in the middle of the ride
change who you are inside
you're the only one that can

change planets

i am just popping over to Jupiter
thinking of moving there
nice this time of year
or so they say

change places in space
change your place in time

change race

change lanes
change lives
change speed
change direction

change back to when i was young
again
change changes me
i see it
change me
chains of change
aligned
lined up like a freight train
moving through me
making changes as my whole world rearranges me
again

change colours
change planes
change levels of awareness
change opinions
change minds
change jobs

change your own expectations
change nations
change the constitution
change religion
change religions
change the world
change of scene
seen the world change

change means renewal as well as decay
change today
change of heart
change the way
you feel you play your part

change where you always go
change everything you know

change tables
change angles

changing points of view will reveal the big picture

change of style
change angels to ease us through change would be nice

change the tyres
change track
change the process
change the system
change it back
a gain?

change the sheets

changing beats
change repeats
change repeats
change repeats

everything changes

nothing

i am quite excited about writing this down said rat

i like the way that sits on the page said ant

here

there is nothing there
all I have is here
here inside
inside me
my reality

there
is a void
i avoid
an abyss
of emptiness
there
is nothing there

if i look in
i miss all this
here
outside me
my reality

a world of broken hearts
and unfair lives
gives rise to anger
hatred
fear
a void
and empty feelings

there
is no reason
clearly
no answer to the question why
knowing answers doesn't fill the void

here
i am alive
here is where i thrive
survive
live

time

time resonates
fast slow
past always
leaving

space relates

limited infinite
future storage
extra baggage

matter of fact
matter of action
moving in
   now
solid out
   still
present danger
fear of
loss

losing balance

mind
———
matter
equates to
time
and space to
enjoy this state
of
mine

About the Author

Tony Piggott is a New Zealand artist/retired ad guy whose life has had many iterations. Business owner, artist, actor, writer, traveler are all terms that apply.

Currently he is also dad to two teenaged daughters who can rightfully blame him and his very lovely and clever wife for dragging them all over the world and being unable to settle.

Ruth Sterlin

Introductory Words

My writing has changed since we published *Wednesdays with Winston* in 2018. Until then, it was driven by a wish for finely honed prose and correctness. While it was fun, and friends shared their enjoyment of my essays, I soon entered a long period of not writing at all. I was sure that my creative well had run dry.

One day, while tapping the computer keys, typing anything that came to me, words about suicide, depression and all kinds of human pain emerged on the page. This is the heart of life, I thought! I had finally kicked down the fence of correctness. To my surprise, the pieces I've written since then have been unexpectedly diverse, not only describing the dark side of life, but also containing humor, weirdness and even musicality in the form of poetry. I invite you for a wild ride —alternating between sweetness and despair, depression and hope, seriousness and absurdity. Enjoy your trip!

My Own Jiminy Cricket

Lately, I've had a hard time writing. Prose, essays, poetry, it's all been escaping me. Then, late last night, I finally figured it out! I'm being followed by Jiminy Cricket. Everywhere I go, I look back and there he is. Sometimes, he even parks himself on my shoulder. Actually, this has been going on for a very, very long time. All of my life, actually.

I haven't stolen him from Pinocchio. My Jiminy Cricket is not at all like his. Mine's more of a Yussel Cricket, since instead of a top hat he has a *kipa* perched on top of his gray hair. He limps because of a recent hip replacement, and he speaks with a slight Yiddish accent. The biggest difference between the two of them is that while Pinocchio's failed to keep him on the straight and narrow, mine has succeeded so well I've become a perfectionist.

This has really affected my writing. For years, I've been hearing his voice as he takes me to task for writing a boring piece, an uninspired essay, or a poem that doesn't quite flow. Sometimes, he complains that my topic is too grim, too short, too distant from my own voice. The list goes on and on. At times, I wonder if my Jiminy Cricket has been the spokesman for my family, since I grew up in a house full of Jewish anxiety and messages like *be cautious, watch your back, don't live on the corner, whisper when you say the word 'Jewish'.* He's surely been influenced by my family who needed all of us to be high achievers, straight A students, Phi Beta Kappa's,

Fulbright Scholars, lawyers who argued before the Supreme Court. That list goes on and on, too.

As I approach my seventy-fifth birthday, I'm still struggling to find a middle ground between serious self-depreciation and total wonderfulness. Jiminy, you've been no help at all! Every time I sit down to write, you point out missing commas, awkwardly constructed sentences, and outright stupid ideas. You've pushed me to the edge, and I am issuing you a warning. Jiminy, beware!

Just when you're not expecting it, I'm going to sneak up on you in the middle of the night. You'll be snoring away, dreaming of fireflies and old loves when I plunge a knife into your tiny heart. I don't know if there'll be blood, since you're a cricket, but this will be murder. Given my background, I'll probably feel horribly guilty, too.

I can promise you though, Jiminy, that after you're dead, I'll lay you out and clean your body respectfully. I have a beautiful spot picked out for your burial in our garden right behind the orange marigolds that are now in full bloom, and I'll say Kaddish for you every Yom Kippur.

I ask for your forgiveness ahead of time. Please understand that, although I'm not a very observant Jew, I believe very strongly in the importance of *tikkun olam,* fixing the world a little at a time. I always try to help people, to be a good listener, to donate food and money to those in need, to be non-judgmental, and to keep my house clean – at least the kitchen and bathrooms. Your murder will be a form of *tikkun olam.* Think about it. It will provide *sholom bayit,* peace in the home. No longer shaken by all of your criticism, I will be much kinder to my poor husband who's spent a lifetime watching me obsess over doing things perfectly. I'll also be a better mother to my children, freeing them to contribute more to our world. And I'll be more confident flipping our President the bird when he behaves badly. Let's face it, Jiminy. After you're gone, the world will be a better place – and I'll write more!

So, let us begin our goodbye, even if it makes us both cry

and wring our hands. I hope you'll find comfort in my faith that, after your death, you'll go to heaven or wherever people and crickets go when they die. Somewhere in that Great Beyond, there's gotta be someone who needs you more than I do.

Slipping on the Ice

I reach straight back in time, as if to melt
the ice that day my body hit the ground,
take back my slipping toe, the pain I felt,
the fear I had outrun life's clock, the sound

a shriek, a shattered bone that hung askew.
Take back the day's spent hours on a gurney,
the sterile drip, the dizzy bruising hues,
and questions on the reason for my journey.

When small, my tears and smiles vied for sun
with bouncing, falling, hard to tell apart,
afloat with dreams that I could never run
aground where breathless sand can stop the heart.

Now dots and flashes hot behind my lids
grow flowers on the ice to soften memory,
allowing me to heal, to find the gift
of solid ground, the point of life in me.

"A ring when it's rollin'..."

It was less than a week after my sister died, way too soon to start cleaning out her apartment. Unfortunately, her daughter and I live in different cities, and we had no choice but to tackle this dreary task right away. The bedroom was especially difficult, since my sister had been moved to the living room for her final days under hospice care. If ever there were a dark cloud, it was knowing that she couldn't even spend her last night in her own bed.

So how does a person figure out where to start? The closet? The shelves? I decided to sit down in front of her dresser. Reluctantly, I opened the top drawer. Inside sat a tangle of necklaces, earrings and watches. My sister had a keen eye for jewelry, and what she couldn't buy in precious jewels, she made up for in artistic flair with colorful pieces she would find in thrift stores and consignment shops. I recognized one brightly colored necklace from our trip together to Mexico. My sister had invited me to spend a week with her in her timeshare on the coast, and between downing margaritas and going on day trips, we visited a small shop where she bought this string of colored beads for a pittance.

My niece called from the other room, "Take whatever you want from there." I thanked her, but I didn't really want any of it. I didn't need anything, and it was all just too sad. Sorting through the mass in front of me, I thought I saw something sparkle. I looked closer. There was my mother's wedding ring! I couldn't believe it. My niece had assured me that it was in a safe deposit box at the bank, but here it was right in front of me, the ring my mother had worn for decades before it was passed down to my sister. I quickly rescued it from the clutter. "Maryam, you're not going to believe what I found!"

My niece came in and sat down beside me. "Try it on," I said, handing it to her. "You should have this." Wide-eyed, she took the ring from me. Because she is large-boned, it wouldn't fit either of her ring fingers. Not even her pinky could slip inside since all of her fingers were very wide. "Here, you take it," she said as she handed it back to me.

While the ring felt very light in my hand, it also carried the weight of years of memories. My mother designed it herself: one large diamond surrounded by two parentheses of tiny diamonds all set into a wide, gold band. When she was nearing her sixtieth birthday, I remember her asking my father for a ring with diamonds. She'd worn a tiny silver wedding band since the day they got married. As I think about it now, there was a lot behind her wish for a new diamond ring. Perhaps, having diamonds on her wedding ring finger made her feel more a part of the world, more like her friends. She'd grown up in an immigrant family that came to America from Turkey. She also lost her mother at a very young age. In grade school, she took out the pierced earrings that had been in her ears since birth. There were so many ways in which she felt different from other girls.

When the ring was ready, my mother invited me to sit next to her on her bed while she rolled it back and forth on her hand to make the diamonds catch the light. I was excited for her. At 27, I was far enough along in my own life to understand that, given the poor background she came from, getting this ring meant a lot to her. My father must have also understood that her request for this ring with diamonds carried a lot of weight. Ordinarily, he didn't hesitate to look for ways of cutting corners when it came to paying for things. He scrimped on carpet measurements when we got a new carpet for our family room, and he griped constantly about syna- gogue dues. Getting him to pay for anything outside of what he considered a necessity aggravated him no end. I witnessed endless arguments between my parents over money. In retro- spect, it makes sense.

My parents started out their marriage on the heels of the Great Depression with almost no money. First, they lived with my father's mother. My mother hated that living arrange- ment and would walk for hours on end pushing my sister in a baby carriage just to get out of the house. Not long after my sister was born in 1936, they moved to the Jane Addams sub- sidized apartments, a relatively new Chicago project. When my own children were babies, my mother would tell me on phone calls about how trapped she felt during the Chicago winters in that tiny little apartment, unable to get out even to buy groceries. My father was exempt from going off to war. As the sole support of his own mother, my mother and my older sister, he drove a delivery truck during the day barely making ends meet. Having a car for my mother to use was out of the question.

I always wondered if my mother's new diamond ring helped her sweep away memories of the many hardships in her spartan past, of growing up with only two dresses hang- ing in her closet – both hand-me-downs, of the years of caring for small children on my father's small salary. When she died at 88, I confess that I really wanted her diamond ring. Envi- ous, I made peace with the decision that it should go to my sister. Of course. She was the oldest, and it should be passed to her. That was the end of it, at least I thought it was.

Imagine the amazement I felt finding out that this diamond ring would end up on my hand. My sister is gone, but the ring goes on, like the ring in the children's lullaby that "...*when it's rollin' it has no end.*" It now sits on my finger. As much as I love this ring, though, its presence there carries a certain weight. The reasons for this are very different for me than they were for my mother.

Partly in reaction to the fights over money during my childhood, by the time I was a teenager, my mission in life was to rebel against having lots of possessions. When I went off to college, I packed a big suitcase and three large cardboard boxes. I told my mother she could get rid of everything else I owned. She just looked at me like I was crazy, but that's a story for another time.

During the sixties, I was particularly outspoken about the plight of the poor. My long hair, bell bottoms and sandals were my world, and I disparaged all forms of wealth. When we hit the seventies, I hadn't changed much but I decided to move in with my boyfriend who had a one-bedroom apartment. Still protesting against wealth and injustice, I felt sure that I would've been content living in a cardboard box. I taught school on the south side of Chicago and, outside of chocolate chip cookies and transportation to work, I couldn't have cared less about *things*. Eventually, my boyfriend and I decided to get married. Together, we went to pick out my engagement ring: a simple gold ring with a single garnet, soon to be accompanied by a thin gold wedding band. A diamond was the last thing I wanted.

During the entire time I was raising young children and establishing my career as a social worker, I gave my wedding ring very little thought. Simple was always best for me. Yet, when I reached my mid-sixties, I began to recognize a vague wish to have a diamond wedding band. Who would have ever thought? To this day, I am at a loss to explain it. Was my mother somehow communicating something to me from wherever she was? Or maybe just wanting something that she had wanted made me feel close to her.

My husband was mixed about this new turn in my thinking. It's possible he wasn't happy about the fading of my hippy streak. I also believe he wanted me to continue wearing the ring I had worn every day of our marriage, with the exception of one day of childbirth for each of my two children. Even so, when my mother died and her ring eventually came to me, he was able to agree to the exchange of my original wedding band for my mother's. Like my father, he came through, understanding my wish to feel connected to my mother by wearing her ring. I am very grateful, partly for his caring response, and partly because it has shown me that some very good things in my family life have been passed down from one generation to the next.

I've been wearing my mother's ring for over a year now, and I've noticed something. Every so often this wonderful, sparkling ring starts to feel very heavy on my finger. The magical part of me wonders if my mother is pulling on it to remind me of her. Does she want it back? Or is it my sister who's doing the pulling. This ring has outlived two very important women in my life. When it feels too heavy, I put it back in my dresser drawer and replace it with the wedding band from my husband. Then, when the diamond ring is no longer on my finger, my mother and my sister can have it back for a while.

Magic

A hungry virus sweeps into a pile
the fragments of my plans, plane reservations
ripped in two, and gobbles with a smile
torn-up dreams of having a vacation.

My skin is bruised with inactivity
and time drips through my veins from head to heel.
Granddaughter blows me kisses through the screen
with hugs and tickles we pretend to feel.

Don't let her see the bodies piled in trucks
to cool the hands that once could share a bowl,
the beast on wheels engorged with human husks,
the questioning if leaders have a soul.

Just let her wave the magic wand she got
for her eighth birthday party that I missed.
She points it at me, scowls and says, "It's NOT
a toy!!" Of course. I know it's real, I insist.

She scatters spike-winged monsters with a frown
and swishes air to ply her wizard craft–
"The dragons fly away, I scare them now!"–
then melts into a smile when I laugh.

Ruth Sterlin

Her wand can't wake the bodies in the truck
or stop the virus sucking up our lives.
Her real magic happens when I'm stuck,
turns pain to giggles, keeping me alive.

Out of the Dark Corner

Recently, I opened an email from a high school classmate. As I began to read it, I was totally unprepared for what he'd written. His son had just committed suicide. How horrible! He was thirty-five years old and had suffered from serious depression all of his young life, struggling mightily with hospitalizations and never-ending ups and downs. Along with shock and sadness, what really struck me was that this friend, a pastor, chose to share all of this in a group message to the forty of us who have kept in touch since our fiftieth high school reunion. He *wanted* to talk about it, to bring it out in the open. He made it clear that his son's suicide will not be hidden in a dark corner.

Whether I'm working with psychotherapy clients or out with friends, I see how even mentioning the word *suicide* makes people lower their eyes or go freshen their drink in the next room. You certainly won't hear about it at *Story Jam*. Even so, its specter hovers around us more than we know – in the people we love, in those we work with, even within ourselves.

I understand why people shy away from the word. Someone taking their own life by drug overdose, hanging, gunshot wound, or any other horrific act that a desperate human being can think of? Of course, no one wants to hear about it. There's nothing poetic or romantic about it – just crushing violence, followed by silence. Except in rare circumstances, it means they gave up. They extinguished their flame with their own hand. It's terrifying, especially for those of us who've been tempted ourselves.

Yet, my classmate's courage in writing us all this email was actually helpful. For me, it reinforced the truth that we can learn and grow from having these stories come out in the open. It gave me courage to tell my own story.

Like my friend's son, I also suffer from depression. It's taken me many years to understand that it's not my fault, just dumb luck that makes me fall into a very dark place, BAM! No warning. Like a deep pothole that appears out of nowhere and wrecks my tire. Good luck is when the pothole isn't deep enough to total the entire chassis.

Depression kicked in full force during my adolescence. I felt sad all the time, at home, at school, even when I was out with friends. It was a time in my life when I was trying to figure out who I was and, more importantly, who was *there* for me. I felt very isolated, a feeling that only intensified because I believed I shouldn't feel this way, and I definitely shouldn't tell anyone how much I was suffering.

One day when I was sixteen, I found myself standing in front of the medicine cabinet in our upstairs bathroom. I remember that it was summer, because I had on a sleeveless blouse. No one else was home, and I really didn't know what I was doing there. When I opened the cabinet, all kinds of bottles stared out at me. Some were brown with pills in them. Some were clear with different colored liquids. There were very large bottles, and some were so small I couldn't imagine them holding anything of importance. Picking up each one, I read the fine print on the back. Mostly, there were lists of ingredients and cautions about keeping the medicine away from small children. There were also dosage indications over the names of doctors. What was going on in my head? I don't recall thinking anything – just a kind of numbness – but I knew that overdoses could kill you. For a moment, everything came to a stop. Time stood still. Then, slowly the thought of killing myself began to crystallize. Did I really want to die? Maybe. Probably. When I couldn't settle on any particular bottle, my eyes moved away from them to my father's razor resting just above.

The razor had a shiny metal handle with a platform casing at the top to hold the razor blade. When I twisted the handle, the casing opened to release the blade. My father kept it sharp, because he had a tough beard, and on this particular day, only five hours had gone by since he had used it. When I was younger, I would often watch him shave, carefully removing every last whisker and speck of shaving cream from his cheeks. Standing there now, I had a fleeting memory of how smooth his cheeks felt when he kissed me goodbye on his way out the door.

My father suffered from depression, too. So did his mother. Talk about a gift that gets handed down from generation to generation. His mother, my grandmother, was pretty scary. I experienced her as a woman with angry, frizzy hair who rarely spoke to me. When we would visit her, she'd grasp my father's arm.

"Don't leave me, Mel!" she would cry.

In the end, she found her own way of giving up, of extinguishing her flame: she sat for hours in her armchair looking through the only clean spot at the center of her window, watching people walk by. Thankfully, setting an example that probably saved me, my father's depressions reached a point where, after a while, I would hear him say that *dammit he wasn't going to be like his mother and stay inside all day*. And then he would get himself out of bed, shower and shave.

Which brings me back to the razor. I took the blade out of the razor and placed it between my thumb and forefinger. I had no idea how people actually slit their wrists. *Just do it*, I thought. Holding the blade tightly, I swiped it over my inner left wrist. The blade didn't even break the skin. Terrified and determined, I did it again, harder. This time it drew blood. I stopped, shocked. Maybe I didn't really want to die, and maybe my family would miss me. I put the blade in the razor and slid it back on to the shelf. Closing the cabinet door, I saw my lost, frightened face in the mirror. I didn't know how but somehow I had to find a way to go on, and that it was better to be standing up than lying bleeding on the floor. How lucky I was to come to that resolve. It could have turned out very differently. How tragic for those who aren't so lucky.

For a long time after that day, I blamed my family for my pain. Where was everyone at that terrible moment in my life? Why wasn't someone looking out for me? The fact is that my sister was away at school, my brother was out with friends, and my parents were both at work; but even if they had all been there with me in front of the medicine cabinet, I'm not sure it would've helped. Sadly, emotional supplies in my family were in short supply. Over time, I came to understand that my mother had lost her own mother when she was only fifteen months old. My father was brought up by my depressed grandmother, whose emotional state was made even worse by the stillborn child she'd given birth to before my father was born. The constant arguments between my parents, and my older brother joining in with his loud voice, were signs that, for the most part, all of us were just hanging on by our emotional fingernails. And, no one ever talked about it. For me, the worst part of that painful episode is that I never told anyone about my brush with my father's razor. If I had, maybe I could have gotten help. Maybe it would have changed the course of my entire life.

I will never judge someone for taking their own life. I know what it feels like to be in a dark, blinding cloud with no hope of a solution, or a hurricane where you can't see anything as you grope for a branch or a tree, anything that's twisting in the wind so you won't blow over. Hope lies in knowing that dialogue about human problems and about suicide has opened up a lot during the past decade or so, and that these conversations will save many lives. I grieve for my high school classmate. What could be worse than losing a son through suicide?

At the same time, I want him to know that by sharing the truth of how his son died, he helped me feel permission to tell my story. I think he has helped everyone on our email list by using the word *suicide,* and making us talk about it.

Nickels from Heaven

At security, I sign in with a fake name. I don't want anyone to know I'm here for a therapy appointment. Okay, I admit it. I tell my own therapy clients that going to therapy is nothing to be ashamed of, but this morning I'm sure someone's going to take one look at me and know: she's neurotic, she's here for therapy. The lobby is packed. I pray I won't run into anyone I know, especially a client, *godforbid*. If I had my way, I'd beam myself up into the chair in my therapist's office so no one would even see me. Ruth, calm down. Physician, heal thyself.

Her office is on the sixth floor, but I'm early so I head for the cafeteria on the second floor to grab some breakfast. I've been there before, and I always sit at one of the tables in the back and face the wall. As I come out of the elevator, I see how full the cafeteria is. But I'm hungry, so I grab a tray, a bran muffin and a cup of black coffee. I also take a wad of extra napkins, just in case… well, you never know when you might need them.

Wouldn't you know it, the line to the cash register is long and slow. I feel like giving the cashier my cup of coffee so she'll speed up the line. The line inches forward and I spend time looking at the ceiling, the floor – God, this is taking forever – then my watch. Only ten minutes until my appointment. At last, I reach the cashier.

"Four fifty-three," she says in a monotone. *You really took your time, lady,* I think to myself since by now I'm really irritated. I want to maintain a cool exterior, so I balance my tray on the counter and reach in my purse for the five-dollar bill I grabbed on the way out the door this morning. I rummage. Kleenex, keys, old candy, lip balm, but no fiver. Oh, God! What if I don't have it, what if it fell out of my purse. I'm sure I put it in my purse. What if I've been standing in this damned line for nothing?

Trying to regroup, I take a deep breath and look down at the floor where there's a repairman fixing some wiring below the cash register. He's bent over working his screwdriver with his shirt hiked up and his pants drooping low, way too low. My eyes happen to land on that infamous crack staring up for all to see.

Surprised, I jerk my head up, and suddenly, I am in a slow-motion movie. My purse slams into my tray, my cup tips over and hot coffee spills – you guessed it – right into this poor man's nickel slot. He grabs his behind with both hands and bellows, "OWWW!" Every head in the cafeteria turns to stare at me and the man hollering his lungs out. I exhale so intensely, my lungs empty out. Couldn't the floor *puhleez* just open up and swallow me whole? In a daze, I toss the man my wad of extra napkins and hightail it out of the cafeteria.

I head for the stairs without looking back. Forget the elevator, my adrenaline kicks in and I run up four flights of stairs as fast as I can. By the time I reach my therapist's office I am so winded, I have to stop in the hallway to catch my breath. At this point, I don't even care if anyone sees me in front of her office. So what if they know I'm here for therapy? What's the big deal? At least they won't know about the disaster downstairs in the cafeteria!

Morning Brew

My head turns just in time to catch a glimpse
of me in slippers coming down the stairs.
Each foot feels for grounding while I wince
at aches that show up silently in pairs.

I check my face for smiles or tears or signs
of giving up life's climb as I descend,
and watch me head for breakfast since it's time
for smells of morning brewing its hot blend.

Strands of gray startle my reflection
in the kitchen window as I peek
outside to see if morning has the gumption
to show up, to never skip a beat.

Questions stir like Prufrock's coffee spoon
about the day and what it will turn up,
why dancing with my chestnut curls has gone
to memories in the soapsuds with my cup.

The devil in me laughs – how life's terrain
can steepen sharply just as strength goes down
like hearing aids that tumble in the drain!
Yet passion keeps me singing songs out loud....

About the Author

Ruth Sterlin is a psychotherapist and a writer. During her career as a clinical social worker, she has published several articles in professional journals. Over time, her writing interests have turned to personal essay, memoir, and, more recently, poetry. Ruth lives with her husband in Glenview, Illinois, and has children and grandchildren spread throughout the country. She looks forward to being able to travel again to visit them all after the pandemic has settled down. In the meantime, when she is not working or writing, she enjoys listening to classical music, doing yoga, riding her bicycle and avoiding housework. Ruth says that she has always loved to write, because, in the words of Anne Frank, "Paper is patient." … and thankfully so.

Anne Sylvan

Anne Sylvan

Introductory Words

In poetry class I hear "Trust the process." This is advice I've gotten before, and advice that I've learned to heed.

Two of these poems grew from both the liberty of a class free-write, and the constraint of a poetic form or feature. The third poem is a recollection of place — homage to a city in which I had the good fortune to dwell.

Anne Sylvan

Octopus Encounter: A Ghazal

Like the snakes on Medusa's head, eight willful arms
grope with rubbery reach at the urge of octopus.

Eight dissonant limbs unwind to stretch and tap. Then drift
and retreat, to regroup and converge as one tangled octopus.

Now startled! The two-eyed head bolts as if shot from a
     cannon
trailing eight arms like a jet stream behind a surge of
     octopus.

Only to slow, then settle on coral rock terrain. In a
     photographic flash
skin morphs-vanishes to a coral-rock guise, a purge of
     octopus.

It's a gambol, and Anne's Ramble. It's a two-eyed globe
     with eight limbs
that scuttle away. Eight consonant limbs that diverge as one
     octopus.

A Wannabe Wordsmith

A tack hammer tool
   not a bruiser sledge
   but a spare Brancusi form
   with two crusader arms held aloft

When a tune sprang from its head
   the hammer excused itself
   from pushing things around
It wished to be draped

Draped with a cape
   that passed through a child's ring
The cape's murmur so fine
   it displaced barely an exhalation as it

   arced the hammer into the sky and
   bolted like a cross bow kite
The wood tool windwhistling   the
   cape spinnaker gleaning   stars

   upstart stars
   stars ready to confabulate
   a glitter track   a comet tail

Anne Sylvan

Whether a tale unhinged   or at long last loose
   even keenly sounds reverb in the hammer's
   head   the interior pungent
   with lilac's spring

A caped crusader
driving a dark night dazzle
tooling a windfall of light

Jerusalem
City of Peace
and
Curiosity

I wandered in weather temperate
I wandered in blast furnace heat and icy drizzle
Forty years ago   I wandered along lanes
    lined with tall stone walls
Gates flashed open then shut   blinking
    hinting at sanctuary   at courtyard and garden
    palm tree and fountain

I climb to Golgotha   once a hill top   now a mezzanine
    illumined by high flocks of oil lamps
The intricate altar   shimmering like a constellation
    in a space dim   a fragrant grotto   barely illuminated
where wall floor and ceiling may never meet
    big-bearded pale monks chant there
    some times

Anne Sylvan

I return to the main floor   to the Stone of the Anointing
the Stone of Unction
A line of oil lamps hovers   glowing over
the slab rubbed smooth by pilgrims
rubbed smooth with fragrant oils
I touch the stone   my fingers now fragrant
with I know not what

Beneath the dome I see the Edicule
the Lilliputian tomb-shrine
a glow issues   golden from the elfin entrance
it holds six pilgrims and two stern monks
there's a line
there's always a line
I don't wait

I go outside   Climbing up I turn left
and left again
then a third left   into the lane
with the bone-plain grey metal gate at the end
It's open

The Russian Compound, Jerusalem

257

I step onto the roof   The Church roof
It's an expanse   a wide plain
　　awash in high desert sunlight
Ethiopian monks and
　　their emerald green huts are here
the monks   tall narrow and dark
　　glide rather than stride
　　their motion effortless
otherworldly

I wander into the Ethiopian Chapel
Murals of Biblical scenes   out-of-doors scenes
　　in impossibly vivid blocks of color
　　cover the walls
There is the Queen of Sheba
　　coming down the Nile
　　to meet King Solomon

This is a Christian aerie
　　but as I gaze
The scenes harken to
something older
something wider

I daydream it into tribal veneration
an African celebration of what is vivid and alive
about their place
their story

an Origin Story

brought along with care
from we know not where

About the Author

Anne Sylvan was born in Chicago. She left for fifteen years and happily returned. She writes about creatures, human and otherwise, along with places and things. Anne came to poetry only three years ago and is glad she did.

Judy SooHoo

Introductory Words

I am slowly making up for lost time. When I was young, I enjoyed creative writing. Then reality took over and business writing became the norm. In my retirement, I ventured into my long-lost interest. My first class was in personal essay and memoir because the creative writing class I wanted to take was full. But this led me fortuitously to my supportive writing circle and the stories I needed to give voice to — ones of loss and identity.

Through the encouragement of Donna Pecore of the Budlong Woods Writers, I have discovered an entirely new realm of expression in poetry, much of which is informed by current events. My exploration of these topics has been warmly embraced by Janise Hurtig, of the Community Writing Project, to whom I am also deeply grateful.

Auntie

She was my mother's counterpart, Auntie to me, but not blood relation, and a person who played a strong role in my childhood. She was one of those people who made you feel included and important in the world of grown-ups just by looking directly into your eyes. As a young teenager, I experienced that first nascent sense of my own personhood from her, even while being known as my parents' daughter. As more time passed, in the poignant and nostalgic reversal of life, as I would remember her, I wondered if she would still remember me.

My mom and Auntie came from the same village in China. They were grammar school classmates and found themselves settled in the Chinatown neighborhood on Chicago's south side. Her family preceded mine to America as ours fled the Communist takeover in the mid-1950s.

It was not an opulent world, but one of freedom and opportunity found through the hard work of young families. This was accompanied by the relief of having escaped a violent and oppressive government. Both my parents worked: my father in the laundry and restaurant businesses and my mother at a sewing factory, and at home, delicately hand embroidering linen pieces. Back then, latchkey kids and playing in the neighborhood streets until dark were the norm.

But there were differences between the two women. Auntie was short at less than five feet tall and of solid build with a round, freckled face made even rounder by short, loose, curly black hair that started high on her forehead and framed her crown. She was boisterous, full of life with an air of confidence, and took pleasure in making you agree with her in a jovial way. When she made a declarative statement, she would turn to me and ask, "Right, my little girl?"

On the other hand, my mother was taller at five feet, five inches, slim at 90 pounds, and quite attractive. The youngest of six children, she was the demure, playful type, but was at times childishly mean, enjoying other people's misfortunes. Auntie was a little older than my mother and forgave her behavior, graciously taking on her role as big sister and protector of us both. But there was another distinction that created a special bond between Auntie and me. She had a raucous brood of four sons, a gender that Asian culture prized. Even so, Auntie would always say how lucky my mother was to have a girl allowing her to unabashedly dote on me.

Auntie lived in a cramped space rigged as an apartment on the second floor above a gift shop on Wentworth Avenue — one of two main streets in Chinatown. The front area facing the street consisted of a living room, a small kitchen large enough to fit an aluminum dining table, and the parents' bedroom. Movements between the rooms were pronounced by drops in the floor or by the clanking sound of the thin metal thresholds every time you crossed over them. The back of the apartment, which I would only get glimpses of going down the narrow hallway to the bathroom, housed the always active boys' area.

On summer visits, we would be greeted at the top of the stairs with Auntie, a comical sight in pink, plastic, snap-on curlers; a thin, cotton-print, shift dress that belied her seamstress skills; and plastic unisex slippers that would clap each time they would hit the bottoms of her feet. Her welcoming smile shone through all of that. We climbed the long, tight stairway with our bags of fruit, pastries, or other goodies which Auntie always ensured that I had my fill of.

Gatherings with them were like a large, crowded clan meeting which included her mother and in-laws, while I had only my one grandparent. Otherwise, I did not know much about Auntie. But I knew she suffered an early tragedy. Her husband had cancer and back in the '60s, that was a death sentence. It was popular thinking at the time that cancer was contagious but we kept up our visits.

I would enter the lightly draped-off living room and greet Auntie's husband who was tall, by Chinese standards, medium-built and who would be lying on the couch under a light blanket. He was a loud and animated man that had once towered over me. In his attempts to make conversation, he had me at attention looking up, afraid to move. But since his illness, there was little to say aside from the perfunctory greetings, and I was now looking down at him, fearful for him. Visits shortly after he passed left me alone in the empty living room with my parents in the kitchen and a quietly sobbing Auntie.

Subsequent visits were infrequent as we moved to the Northside of the city. I would drive my parents over to her home where the focus of the conversations were her sons and the local gossip. She always greeted me with a smile, happy to see me and remarked, "Such a good daughter!"

Time can find you in many directions away from home. Auntie and her sons moved to a new townhouse at the southern edge of Chinatown. I married and moved to the suburbs. One of our last joyful gatherings was over 30 years ago at my wedding when Auntie's three-year-old granddaughter was my flower girl and her four-year-old grandson, my ring bearer.

I had often thought of calling her and cautiously wondered if she were still alive. Was her number the same? As a child I had dialed it from memory thrilled at being recognized with small talk, as I handed the receiver over to my mother.

I was stunned to hear that Auntie died last Wednesday. Her phone number rolled off my tongue. Now I know that she was indeed still alive and that her number, undialed for so long, was still with me.

The Nine Kinds of Love – For John Lewis

Storge —
familial love for sharecroppers
Willie-Mae and Eddie, parents of 10,
"accepting" of John's calling for
higher learning at school, not farm chores,
freedom, not the safety of his denizen.

Philia —
affectionate love for his many
cousins, nieces, nephews, and friends.
At 21, on buses as a Freedom Rider,
at lunch counters, and sit-ins for the
"Beloved Community" of the nation and its citizens.

Eros —
romantic love for a stylish Lillian Miles.
Wife, advisor, lock-step partner of 44 years —
teacher in Nigeria, Peace Corp volunteer, librarian,
whip-smart of people details, problem solver,
together, hopeful for humanity through their Foundation's
    affairs.

Ludus —
playful love for adopted son, John-Miles.
Love at first sight at two months old, not a moment later

teaching "Learn from the past!"
Embracing hip-hop music of a new generation
enlightened by the struggle recounted in son's song
    "Political Behavior.[1]"

Mania —
John's obsessive love of his farm chickens.
At 15, Emmett Till his George Floyd,
on the radio, Martin Luther King, Jr.
Later "Workhorse not show horse," the "Soul" and
"Good Conscience" of Congress, "Good Trouble" to be
    embroiled.

Philautia —
self-love
organizing a peaceful protest in '65 at 24
barely surviving Bloody Sunday on the Bridge at Selma
that passed the Voting Rights Act,
that Obama wrote on his Inaugural Day, "Because of you,
    John" his mentor.

Agape —
self-less, universal love,
proud of his 40-some arrests
many times beaten, risking life and limb.
To Act — complicit, if tolerated – a silent tour-de-force
against those who fought and opposed him in protest.

Pragma —
enduring love
for Gandhi's non-violence
for Douglass' equal justice
for all the oppressed
of the past and the present.

And, Unio Mystica —
a return to the historied, blue-signed Ebenezer Baptist
    Church[2]
iconic of leaders and martyrs in the guiding light of truists.
Laid now to fitting rest at South-View[3] where MLK was first
    buried[4]
and black slaves and their free, first-born lay in dignified
    godspeed.
Storied to all, mystical with God, John Lewis.

---

1   Chu, Louise. "Staging Their Own March." *Washington Post*, 18, Jan 2004, digital archives. "Political Behavior" was a hip-hop song written by John-Miles recounting his father's and other activists' struggle in the civil rights movement that changed John Lewis' mind about his son's choice of a music career

2   Suggs, Ernie. "Ebenezer Baptist Church fitting site for John Lewis' funeral." *The Atlanta Journal-Constitution*, 29, July 2020, digital edition. Ebenezer Baptist Church where John and Lillian were members, their marriage officiated by Rev. Martin Luther King, Sr., and where Martin Luther King, Jr. was co-pastor

3, 4   Toone, Stephanie. "What to know about the place where John Lewis will be buried." *The Atlanta Journal-Constitution*, 29, July 2020, digital edition. South-View Cemetery founded by nine black businessmen for the dignified burial of black slaves who at the time were segregated in cemeteries; visitors were required to go through the back-gate wading through swampy land; and in response to "If you don't like it, start your own cemetery."

Profile in Black

37 stops
16 shots score the goal
Laquan McDonald
41 shots attempted by four
Amadou Diallo
12 shots for penalties
Michael Brown

37 stops
1 shot for a shoot-out until sudden death
Trayvon Martin
1 plastic bag over the head for rain delay
Sandra Bland
50+ baton twirls in the air
Rodney King

37 stops
Chokehold wins the takedown
Eric Garner
Spinal cord injury ends the game
Freddie Gray
A mother and child watches from behind the paint
Philando Castile

37 stops
Out-of-bound plays stop the clock but not the game
Balls fly and pucks whiz through the air
Deep into the crowd
37 stops too many

Note: 37 stops is one black man's account of how many times he has
been racially profiled and stopped by police.

Judy SooHoo

Profile in Black Updated: For George

She lovingly tends to her flourishing garden
a stalwart to all needs that arise
adapting to whims of weather and wildlife
on hands and knees sowing rich earth

He diligently works on his refuge, his home
fixing things high and low that go wrong
from age, overuse or by fault
on hands and knees striving to achieve

The family sings praises of glory in worship
good deeds to be done throughout
bounties to be returned tenfold
hands and knees supplicating for blessings

Struck down by pain of news to our core
we cry out for help, sweet god
or when saying our final goodbye
hands clenching, kneeling release to peaceful skies

Throughout the ages, this we have seen
revered knights rewarded
defenders debased in defeat
rolling heads taken at the guillotine

Now, in humble protest of misdeeds
we take a knee

And on that heinous 25th day of May 2020
where no line was drawn

With both hands in each
pocket
Left hand in left pocket
Right hand in right pocket
Power and Impunity
fisted over

Oblivious to his charges
Oblivious to eyes and cries
upon him
Oblivious except for

the warmth at his knees
Left knee on neck
Right knee on back
The weight of his body
atop another
The shifting, pulsing,
throbbing for life
Steady pressure on lungs
deflating
Control over servile body
Before the stillness comes

You know it
You feel it
Like no other as
Flesh to rich earth
Flesh to sweet industry
Flesh to uplifting
transcendence
Flesh from the depths of the
soul to the universe

Flesh to flesh

You felt
the warm stillness of his
lifeless being

You can't say you didn't
You can't say you didn't
feel it

You can't say
You knew not

Silence

January 1, 2020 (New Year's Day). It is eerily quiet early in the city, unlike the fuss and commotion of the preceding night where continuous sirens complemented the customary countdown and bursting color spectrum of eye-candy fireworks in the long-awaited cleansing celebration. Skyscrapers and glass-reflecting towers in black and glossy metal, and off-white, creamy white, and other bland flavors of natural cement stand against a gray, seamless sky. It feels like the morning of an apocalypse instead of the morning after a partied-out night. Even Mother Nature is silent giving no hint of the season — no snow, no swirling play of flakes dancing lightly in the air. The only movement across this landscape comes high above the ground where smoke and steam billow from chimney stacks of seemingly empty buildings. There is no movement in the desolate streets, no perceptible movement within the square box frames of windows. As if bracing for the onslaught of another battle-torn year, people in dreamy slumber are in no hurry to make sense of the world. The chilling silence that fills the space offers a much-needed repose, while inviting any and all to enter.

Spring 2020. The silence of our purview has now been imposed. The pandemic has hustled the world into the DMZ of our abodes. With or without that safety, the aloneness that accompanies such silence near kills not just the body but also the soul. There is little outward change between New Year's morning and now; there is no discernible sound or movement in the streets — just the frozen neon lights that reflect a life from eons ago. The stillness is now accompanied by piercing sirens calling for what is unknown, unfathomable. The square box frames of windows offer steady light into the long night. Some flash at the evening hour signaling support of frontline healthcare workers who silently brave the burden of life and death of a country in their singular hands. There is a deadly silence that behind that revered wall chooses Darwinian, not civilized law — leaving the afflicted, the essential, and their families on their own. We are victims to silenced thoughts whether we want them or not.

Summer 2020. The morning silence is a welcome haven from the aftermath of the violence in the streets from the night before. There is relief in the stillness of the dawn; of things that flutter from the wind or lay lifeless on the ground waiting to be properly discarded. Questioning eyes peer out from the multiple aggressions on the stone-cold prison of buildings and towers. The long smoldering silence of muted unrest starts sizzling to release amidst six-feet, spaced-out lines for human necessities. Spirit overrides risk. It erupts on the streets with voices ripping a path to battered souls that succumb to and assuage the oppressors masked as protectors. Moments marked between oppressor and oppressed that have filled the history of our hundreds-year-old nation connect and resurrect the world through small screens. Simmering to a roiling boil, sirens are accompanied by honking, bullhorns, and shouting. The darkness brings both fire and blistered wounds. Silence unleashes itself whether we want it to or not.

Fall 2020. Silence and dread manifest. They seep in and grow, perplexing and numbing the mind spinning round and around years of unspooling of undoing and deadly sins. They send the spirit into a frenzied hole that clamors to be heard. Unaware of their exact entry like a Trojan horse, eyes from the square box frames peer out to the streets and wonder what and when will be the next attack — physical and or mental, and the merciless torture that accompanies it. The bruising of a sore nation that chooses visceral baseness over cerebral exultation has ignited the unseemly that is underfoot. Boarded-up windows stand ready to sustain further assault. Sheltering in place for months and a day brings about a silence that warrants inspection, that bears witness to our life of meaning and calls out for humanity. Our lives are crafted falsely from external stimuli and we must look within ourselves to set our bearings in the world. Silent selves arise as symbiotic souls in the wake of daylight and tumble out refusing to quietly acquiesce to what is to come.

Silence of the heart
Silence of the tongue
Ever-reaching silence
Silences the soul

Effects

Brimming raindrops bounce
Carrying out their business
Make us see to ours

Rare snowflakes frolic
Cascading icy pinpricks
Call us out to play

Rays of sun consort
Soaking Mother and her buds
Drench us in delight

Cool breezes conspire
Swirling in and swooshing out
Let us breathe carefree

Transcending clouds buzz
Painting canvasses up high
Give us pause to fly

Sprinklings of nature
Gracing us throughout the day
Dance under moonlight

Mahjong with Mother
(or the Games We Play)

"Mahj!" But the cry didn't come from my mother, who in her early nineties can still conjure up dazzling, winning hands of the Chinese tile game with the best of them. It came from a petite, octogenarian Jewish lady friend who had never played the game before. East had met her match with West. And little Miss West's luck was only one of the many inexplicable and never boring times during our weekly mahjong games.

It all started one day when the host of my writing group and little Miss West asked me, "Do you know how to play mahjong? Can you teach us?"

Granted I am Chinese but first generation, American-born, and very much westernized. However, I did grow up watching my parents and their friends play. Having inculcated my young son to mahjong (a rummy-style game of sets of like tiles or runs of tiles), it later became a fun family pastime during my parents' retirement. But I needed my mother's expertise: she was the perpetual winner in the family. "Well, bring her," my friends offered. And thus, weekly mahjong with my mother and my two writer friends began.

The all-day affair would start in the living room of the host's house where eight other women writers and I have met for almost nine years. For the last two, I brought my mother – along with her idiosyncrasies – to bear on the group. First are the treats I bring (mixed or chocolate- or peppermint-dipped nuts), but also "hostess gifts" of paper goods (guest towels or toilet paper – necessities of which my mother is the most frequent user).

During the Chicago winter months, I would escort my mother bundled up in a faux fur-trimmed coat, hat and neck warmer; a handknit scarf; and pink, knit gloves. Underneath the outerwear would be a knit or polyester-filled vest worn over a heavy sweater or a soft flannel top; a cotton turtleneck peeking out at the collar; and a long-sleeved undershirt. Pants and long underwear would complete the ensemble along with thick, fur-lined, black suede boots.

Warmer weather would call for lighter fare but still two layers and a light jacket that she zips up to the neck. While I indulge her penchant for layering, this makes sense given the chill of indoor air conditioning.

My mother would sit quietly in her appropriate season-al regalia at the dining table in the adjoining room. The host would graciously offer drinks and treats. The group would update each other before proceeding to the business of work-shopping the writing. My mother would keep busy with nu-merous trips to the bathroom. Although we've made attempts to entertain her with her favorite TV game shows to watch in the back room, she prefers to sit near us. "More coffee or drink?" the host would ask my mother.

"No," I always interjected, "too much bathroom."

Over time my mother has become more comfortable here. She's adjusted well to the intermittent attention of the sweet-est-tempered mixed breed terrier and an unpredictably fickle cat having lived pet-free all her life. Emboldened, my mother would surreptitiously slip into the seat of the first woman to leave the meeting. When her eyes finally meet mine, my silent glare meets her gaze for having invaded "my" writing group.

Upon our meeting's end and before the mahjong begins, the remaining four of us – the host, Miss West, my mother, and I - would have lunch together. Our first was at Bakers

Square, a family restaurant. The chicken pot pie was a safe bet, I thought, as my brother and I grew up with frozen Swanson pot pies and TV dinners which were always a treat from the quickly-assembled Chinese meals made by our parents who both worked. My mother left all the pieces of chicken sitting at the bottom of the crock dish devoid of gravy and vegetables even though she is not a vegetarian.

Subsequently, I chose other dishes for her, but she would fill up on sides of french fries or bread with butter and jams spooned from the small, packaged restaurant cups. Speaking in Chinese and as discreetly as possible, I would chastise her to eat her main entrée. She would respond by rubbing her stomach indicating that she was full. One time, she playfully placed a six-inch french fry sideways into her mouth with the tips hanging out from each side, horrifying me amidst uproarious laughter from my friends.

My mother speaks little English and rarely speaks at all now. Her primary language is Cantonese Chinese and over her 70+ years of being in America, her words have become laced with English slang and colloquialisms such as 'you know' or 'you know.' Not to miss a beat from my otherwise quiet mother, my friends would invariably ask for a translation when she spoke, and I would judiciously oblige. However, my mother once said, "Velly good, you know," and the host, out of habit, turned to me and asked for a translation.

My mother's eccentricities are due to her dementia from Alzheimer's disease, although she has been stable at an early stage for many years now. On a typical mahjong day she wins most of the games. Most annoyingly, she gloats when winning. She cherishes her dominance of the game with big, sparkling eyes and a wide smile accompanied by an air of smugness. When we tire of her incessant winning, she relishes it more by rubbing her hands together and gushing, "He-he-he."

Little game-playing quirks prompted my friends to ask whether they are newly developed habits or old ones overlooked by my mother's previous game-playing partners. For instance, whenever a game ended, instead of shuffling all the tiles for a new game, my mother would take from the discard pile to complete her deck or hold onto her deck if it were unused during the game. Since there are 144 tiles that each measure 1" x 1" x 1.5", the original set up has the four players assembling a wall comprised of a double row of 18 tiles in front of them which acts as a draw "pile". The tiles are shuffled and the walls are reassembled after every game – something which my mother apparently wanted no part of. The three of us would subsequently knock down whatever tiles remained on her side, requiring her to rebuild her wall. She would respond with pouting lips and a cry of "Chui schlem!" translated to "Mean heart!" And oddly enough, after all the effort is made to shuffle the tiles, duplicate tiles would always manage to appear next to each other.

At times, my two friends and I would be engrossed in conversation stopping the game for a few minutes. The first time this happened, my mother left the table to lie down on the couch. Now she would wait patiently and then ask me whose turn it is. If the game had not resumed in response to her query, she would win the game at her next turn.

But my transgressions have not matched my mother's. One time as I excused myself from the table, my friends informed me at the end of the game, that my mother had looked at my hand of tiles, then put her finger to her lips holding them to a code of silence.

While my mother upholds the Asian crown, little Miss West who grew up in a household of mahjong playing but never learned the game, is the second biggest winner. On the rarest of days, Miss West is the biggest winner. But this is not at all evidenced by her game playing skills. She has trouble seeing the characters written on the tiles; is constantly recounting the tiles she has with light taps of her finger; distracts us as she sings off key at the slightest trigger word; and after a prolonged holdup while swearing to us that she is far from winning, wins in the following turn.

Cries of "Mahj!" roll off her tongue although she has yet to remember the only two terms necessary for play: *seng* and *pung*. Calling either brings the game to an orderly stop allowing the player to take a tile from the discard pile. Instead, her combination move to stop play is to say "Um, um, um" with forefinger up; try to recall *seng* with 'sing', 'song' or 'sang', or *pung*, with all its variations; and then, in desperation, even yell out "Bingo!" Intermittent attempts to name her discarded tiles create yet another plethora of sounds. Finally, the correct word, reminded by the host or me, is called out and repeated three times.

Between the two East-West Queens of mahjong, there isn't much room left for winning by the host or me, which tests the limits of the phrase, "it's not winning that counts." But my host lady friend has a special knack as well. Many a time, as we near the last one or two tiles from the draw pile, it will be her winning tile as if the mahjong gods have not forsaken her.

This is how our mahjong-playing Wednesdays are spent. They are filled with fits of laughter that challenge us to make it to the bathroom in time; conversations laced with gaps in memory; and stiff bodies that need to be loosened from cozy dining room chairs – moments that introduce life's new trials and create a camaraderie for all-you-can-do-is-laugh types of situations as we age. This gratefully includes friends who see my mother as delightful – a sobering yet beautiful gift of a kaleidoscopic lens through which a brief reprieve from an inescapable, suffocating reality can be savored, while time and her disease mercilessly progress. They are Wednesdays full of not only exceptional play but exceptional moments to hold onto.

Mahjong, a hundreds-year old tile game originating in China, was modified and standardized by a group of Jewish women in the US during World War II. The Chinese version is based upon rummy-style play while American maajh is based on random and complex winning tile configurations determined annually by the National Association of Mah Jongg League, based in New York.

About the Author

Judy SooHoo has spent most of her life in Chicago, IL, where she was born. Settled now in the heart of the city, she was a northsider growing up, has strong ties to the southside, and a long history with the beautiful, far western suburb of St. Charles. Retired from corporate life (in the northwestern suburbs), she became part of the "sandwich generation." Judy enjoys all of the arts and traveling (pre-COVID times) with her family in tow.

Acknowledgements

We thank all the instructors and writing groups, past and present, for honing our skills and nurturing the creative soul in each of us.

In particular, we thank Donna Pecore, volunteer facilitator of the Budlong Woods Writers for her time and supportive words; and, to Tom Stark, Branch Manager at the Budlong Woods Chicago Public Library for hosting the Budlong Woods Writers through normal times and extraordinary COVID times via Zoom.

Much appreciation goes to an early teacher, Ellen Blum-Barish of Story Studio, Chicago, and the New Trier Extension for "looking for what pops" in creating our own voices, and from which the original Grant Street Writers was formed.

We would like to recognize The Poetry Foundation for instructing many of our poets in structure and form, as well as in the exploration and development of each in their own writing.

We are also deeply grateful to Jenene Ravesloot, Janise Hurtig, Yvonne Wolf, and elyse koren-camarra for their generous time, skills, support, and encouragement of this book.

Special thanks to Gerry Rogers for giving our book its title.

Much appreciation to Phillip Gessert who patiently and expertly guided us through the world of print and ebook publishing design, and to Kat Wertzler for her early assistance.

And last but not least, we are indebted to Ann Fiegen who has graciously welcomed us writers into her Grant Street home for so many years.